THE LEGEND OF DESMOND HOWARD

WRITTEN BY
BILL ROOSE & BOB DUFF

One in a series by

PRESERVING SPORTS HISTORY ONE STAR AT A TIME

Champions Press, LLC
I WORE 21: THE LEGEND OF DESMOND HOWARD

This book is available to purchase in quantity at a special discounted price for your group or business or promotional use. For information, please write to:

Champions Press, LLC
Special Markets Division
30230 Manhattan Street
Saint Clair Shores, Michigan 48082

Many of the photographs for this publication were acquired through the Desmond Howard Family Collection, The University of Michigan Bentley Historical Library (Greg Kinney); University of Michigan Athletic Department (Joe Arcure, Duane Black, Bob Kalmbach, Per Kjeldsen and Barry Rankin); Getty Images Photo Service (Paul Michinard); AP Photo Archives (Matt Lutts); D.I.G Photographics (Dave Reginek); Lake County News-Herald (Mark Podolski); Astor & Black (Omar Vega); Long Beach State Media Relations (Roger Kirk); and Heisman Trophy Trust (Rob Whalen), except where noted. Every reasonable attempt was made to give proper credit. If there is an error, please notify the publisher and a correction will be made in subsequent editions.

Special thanks: Dave Ablauf, Mitch Albom, Joe Bonnell, Barb Cossman, Dan Dykhouse, Felix Gatt, Joe Gatt, Mike Gormely, Richard T. Hewlett, Scott Hirth, Chuck Klonke, Hunter Lochmann, Bruce Madej, Jordan Maleh, Mike Pozsgai, Lynn Roose, Kevin Roseborough, John Storey, Jim Tepel, Paul Treder, and T.J. Weist.

Very special thanks: Hattie Charles, J.D. Howard, Desmond Howard, Jonathan Jones Sr., Chad Jones, Jermaine Howard, and Rebkah Howard.

Printed in the United States of America
Library of Congress Control Number: 2011911920
ISBN 10: 0-9841347-1-9
ISBN 13: 978-0-9841347-1-7

The I Wore logo is a trademark of Champions Press, LLC.

A special thank you to
everyone who contributed
their memories, pictures and
stories to this book.

I appreciate your efforts, time,
generosity – and most
importantly – your friendship.

– Desmond Howard

FOREWARD
BY GREG HARDEN

The Summer of 1989 was hot and humid. Too hot to be inside an indoor track facility constructed of metal walls and a rubberized floor, and with 1,400 football campers between the ages of 14- to 18-years-old. But there we were, Desmond Howard, myself and another Michigan football player following my 45-minute lecture on the identification and elimination of "Self-Defeating Attitudes & Behaviors".

I was mentally tired and physically exhausted that day, with one mission and one mission only – to go home and recover. But 'the best-laid plans of mice and men' are forever altered by the God of necessity. My life was about to change and the seeds of friendship were sown that afternoon when Des decided to give me an opportunity to share my opinions about his next moves.

Unlike many of his contemporaries, Howard listened and listened intently. Most importantly, he questioned and required you to think beyond the superficial before responding. He wanted to know not only how to thrive in a system that historically was insensitive to the personal struggles of identity. He wanted to know about what made me who I was and what mistakes I had made. He wanted an in-depth analysis of what motivated me and others and what the predictable pitfalls were that he would have to face in the near and distant future.

In addition to all of that, he's funny as hell! He can light up a room with a smile and loves more to laugh with you than to laugh at you. He will talk to anyone about anything, and as I saw him evolve it was not uncommon for him to interview strangers and extract details from them that they would probably not have shared easily.

What I will always remember most about Des are the times he would share a vision or allow me to introduce a different view of things. He was clear as could be following the 'tackle in the end-zone' against Michigan State. If he makes the catch we go on to win. We lost and he vowed to never experience losing a game like that again. If the game was on the line, if the ball was in any way catchable, he was going to make the play. That vision, that resolve, was demonstrated over and over again in the games that followed. He looked smooth as silk making history, and yet many missed his power and drive and hunger because he made it look almost like … like Magic.

It was after the 1996 NFL season when Des said to me, "If we (Packers) go all the way, all you have to do is get there." I got there. And the night before Super Bowl XXXI we were sitting in his room when he told me that he was going to have a game to remember and that he was going to give his team great field position, and that he was going to score a touchdown on special teams, maybe two touchdowns.

I've learned that doubting him is a foolish thing to do, and so I asked him why he was so confident about his projections. Des said that his vision was more fact-based than fantasy. He was confident that the New England Patriots were like most NFL teams and would play special teams with no commitment and no intensity. He went on to say that his coaches were true believers not only in special teams as the critical piece to the puzzle, but in his ability to exploit any team's lack of focus on kick-offs and punt returns. So combine skill and speed with instincts and intellect, and what do you get? Desmond Howard.

He is the perfect mentee transitioned into a true friend and transforming into the next master teacher.

So buckle up all ye faithful fans and soon-to-be fans, and travel through Desmond's world with this amazing book filled with pictures, reports and testimonials creatively written, and painstakingly organized by the artistry of the one and only Bill Roose.

N'uff said,

Desmond with Greg Harden (L) and former Michigan teammate Vincent Washington inside Crisler Arena following the memorial service for Bo Schembechler at Michigan Stadium on September 21, 2006.

21

THE LEGEND OF DESMOND HOWARD

1 THE MAGIC BEGINS

Growing Up in Cleveland, Howard develops into a multi-sport star

From the start, the nickname was appropriate, although as Desmond Howard's stature in sporting circles grew, his handle would grow ironic.

Whatever type of ball you threw at him – whether it was to dribble, catch, or run with it – Howard excelled. He stood out above the crowd and was assigned the most important positions in the field of play on his youth teams.

He was a point guard or shooting guard on the basketball court. A center fielder on the baseball diamond. A tailback and defensive back on the gridiron.

"I played all sports growing up," Howard recalled. "Baseball was the first organized sport that I played, actually being on a real team. I won quite a few trophies in baseball. Center field, that was my best position. I dabbled in other positions a little bit, but my position was center field.

"I ran track, too. I was the most valuable runner at the all-city meet in junior high school."

Soon, it became apparent that one of two sports would lead Howard to a potential college scholarship – basketball or football.

"I loved both of them," Howard said. "But at that time I was probably a little better in basketball. Yet for some odd reason I had more of a passion for football."

It was on the hardwood, however, where Howard garnered his nickname – Magic, after legendary Michigan State and Los Angeles Lakers guard Earvin (Magic) Johnson.

"Correct," said Howard, a Michigan Man who can chuckle at the notion he's nicknamed after a Spartan. "Anybody in that time period who came along and was pretty good in basketball, they called him Magic, because of Magic Johnson."

The Howards lived in a two-story, two-bedroom house on Stockbridge Avenue in Cleveland. Desmond's father, J.D. Howard, was a tool and die maker. His mother, Hattie Charles, ran a day care in one bedroom of the house. Their four sons – Desmond, Jonathan, Chad and Jermaine – slept in the other room in two bunk beds.

"Growing up in Cleveland was great. It was traditional for mom to cook a big meal and we would play football on Thanksgiving. We would play on the snow banks and what not. We would use three front yards and that would be our football field. I was a huge fan of the Pittsburgh Steelers, Mean Joe Greene, and the Steel Curtain. With Desmond being so competitive, he had to be a fan of the Steelers' rivals of the time — the Dallas Cowboys. Of course, Desmond's idol then had to be Tony Dorsett. He mimicked that guy and studied him — and that's before they had VCRs and stopping TV and all of this stuff. He would study what Tony Dorsett would do. And then he would wear that Tony Dorsett shirt and he would never take it off."

JONATHAN JONES
Desmond's Oldest Brother

"We used to almost reconstruct bikes because we were of that tool and die mentality, plus my uncle owned a body shop. And this was at the time when Evel Knievel and 'Wide World of Sports' were popular. We would watch Evel Knievel jump then we would go outside with an ironing board and build a ramp. We would jump the sidewalk squares, and the best guy was the one who could jump the most squares. We eventually got to the point where that was boring so we started putting bodies down there. We would ride as fast as we could, then try to lift the front tip up as far as we could, just like Evel Knievel would. I remember Desmond jumping 12 bodies on that orange banana-seat bike. And it was that Christmas that he got the (AMF) Evel Knievel 10-speed bike. That was huge! The following Christmas he got a Dallas Cowboys dirt bike."

JONATHAN JONES
Desmond's Oldest Brother

DESMOND HOWARD
FUN FACTS

With 138 points in 1991, Howard shattered the Michigan single-season scoring record of
117 points set in 1940 by Tom Harmon, the Wolverines' previous Heisman Trophy winner.

L-R Jermaine, Desmond (then in sixth grade), Jonathan and Chad.

Desmond with his mom and Jonathan.

Jermaine (L) helps celebrate Desmond's ninth birthday.

Grandma Gladys Davis with her grandkids (clockwise from L) Sharon Shockley, Jonathan Jones, Chad Jones, Desmond, Shelly Shockley, Jermaine Howard and Janitta Marbury.

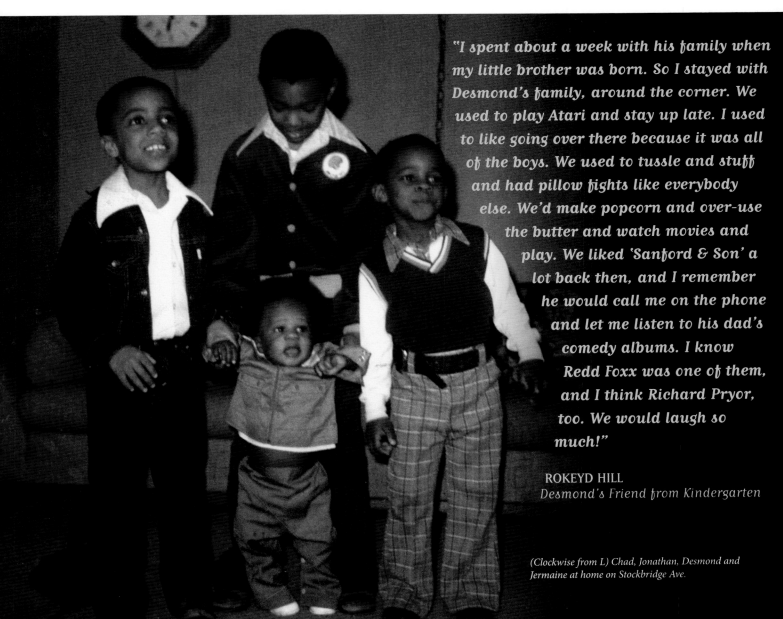

"I spent about a week with his family when my little brother was born. So I stayed with Desmond's family, around the corner. We used to play Atari and stay up late. I used to like going over there because it was all of the boys. We used to tussle and stuff and had pillow fights like everybody else. We'd make popcorn and over-use the butter and watch movies and play. We liked 'Sanford & Son' a lot back then, and I remember he would call me on the phone and let me listen to his dad's comedy albums. I know Redd Foxx was one of them, and I think Richard Pryor, too. We would laugh so much!"

ROKEYD HILL
Desmond's Friend from Kindergarten

(Clockwise from L) Chad, Jonathan, Desmond and Jermaine at home on Stockbridge Ave.

With his family in attendance, Desmond was enshrined in the Greater Cleveland Sports Hall of Fame during a 2005 ceremony. Also inducted that day was former Michigan basketball great Campy Russell. In the background is Bingo Smith, a former NBA star who played from 1969-80, including nine seasons with the Cleveland Cavaliers.

"He's sharp as a tack. He pays attention. He will do his due diligence on any subject. So when you know how he studied me before he came and talked to me — that gives you a clue. He will pay close attention to detail. He will ask the difficult questions. He will ask the questions most people don't want the answers to. He takes criticism better than most.

"The way I saw it — and let's give credit where credit is due — however he was raised, he saw himself being a little bit more than just an athlete. And so my job was to grab that awareness and try to embellish it. His family did an amazing job of keeping him grounded, protecting him from the elements, and by the time that I met him, he was someone who could work with an authority figure, which is usually one of the most difficult pieces in young men, to trust anybody."

GREG HARDEN (ABOVE LEFT)
Michigan, Associate Athletic Director
Director of Athletic Counseling

"My parents divorced and I went to live with my dad," Howard said. "He was kind of my driving force at that point. Coming from a family that breaks up does not dictate that you will become a juvenile delinquent. J.D. and my mother both stressed that you must take responsibility for yourself."

His parents taught Desmond about sacrifice, saving money to allow their children to pursue their dreams. "I owe everything to both of them," Howard said. "I get my humanitarian qualities from my mom. My love of children came from working with her day-care kids. The competitiveness comes from my father. J.D. is an extremist – a competitor who believes you finish what you start."

When they went for walks, Desmond's father would point out thugs on the street. "That's their education right there, learning to sell drugs," he told his son. "And all they will ever get for it is that fancy car. You will never be there, and years from now, they will be right there."

As his high school years approached, the Howards sought out the Cleveland school that might give Desmond the best chance to garner national attention and earn a college scholarship.

"My father and I, we went to a school called Central Catholic to check it out one evening," Desmond remembered. "It was a you've seen this guy play. You've seen some of his films, but I will tell you that this guy was exciting to see in practice. People always ask me, 'What was it like to coach Des?' Now I always had him on the defensive side, because he played free safety for us. And I would say, 'Well, I don't know how much coaching we actually did. But I made sure he was on the bus.' ”

JOHN STOREY
Cleveland St. Joseph
Assistant Football Coach, 1964-94

"I don't think St. Joe's had ever beaten Cardinal Mooney in Youngstown. Des had two touchdowns, three interceptions against them. It was a phenomenal game. There was one third down play and we were on our 44. Bill Gutbrod called 46 Down, which we're running the wishbone, but we were really running the belly. ... Des gets the ball and nobody is blocking anyone, and we had pretty big linemen. Des goes 56-yards. It was the greatest high school run that I ever saw. He made at least three guys miss within five yards of the line of scrimmage.

"After that game was over with, I was standing with him, I hugged him and said, 'Des, I've been lucky my whole life. I played with three Heisman Trophy runners-up (Bob Griese, Leroy Keyes, Mike Phipps) and you're the best I've ever seen.' And you know how he smiles. He just lit up the stadium. When he was accepting the Heisman, do you ever feel in your life like you really called it right? It was just so obvious."

MICHAEL POZSGAI
Cleveland St. Joseph
Assistant Football Coach, 1987-88

Desmond Howard scored a game-high 20-points, including nine in the fourth quarter help lead his recreational team to the Muny Basketball Association championship in 19

"I noticed then that Desmond had a knack for basketball and that he could handle himself pretty good. It was right after he passed through elementary school. He had to be 12 or 13-years-old. When they reached the final game, Desmond had to bring th ball up the court every time. That's when I had saw that he had talent."

J.D. HOWARD
Desmond's Father

MUNY BASKETBALL ASSOCIATION

"*Sometimes we would walk to school together, and there was this one day that I forgot my homework in the house. He climbed up the handrail in the front of the house, onto the awning and through the window and brought the homework out. It just shows his liking for school. He wanted to make sure that I had my homework turned in too. I didn't care too much, but he didn't want me getting in trouble, so he made more of an effort to climb up there. For me, I wasn't about to climb up there; I don't like heights. But it was an example of his fearlessness.*"

ROKEYD HILL (FAR LEFT)
Desmond's Friend from Kindergarten

pretty good school. So we went there to meet with some coaches, check out the school. That night, they happened to be playing Cleveland St. Joseph in basketball, so we stayed for the game.

"We're sitting in the stands, and here comes the St. Joe's basketball team. Back then, the junior varsity would play first, and the varsity would sit in the stands while that game was going on. I watched how St. Joe's came into the arena, just how orderly they were. I liked their attire. They all had on these dark blue blazers, shirts and ties. They sat there and observed. There wasn't a lot of unnecessary activities going on amongst them. There was some of that up in the stands, but they did not participate. I just liked the way they presented themselves.

"I said, 'Daddy, what school is that?' And he said, 'St. Joe's.' I said, 'Let's look into St. Joe's.' And that's how it all started, me going to St. Joe's. Of course, they beat Central Catholic on the court, too. That didn't hurt matters any either. They were impressive on the court. Once we looked into it, we found that this was a school that was a state powerhouse in basketball."

Among the basketball players to come through St. Joseph High were future NBA players Clark Kellogg, Kevin Edwards, Stan Kimbrough and Eric Riley. On the football field, besides Howard, the school also sent his future Michigan teammate Elvis Grbac, brothers Bob and Mike Golic, and London Fletcher to the NFL.

"That's one of the main reasons I went there, because if my athletic ability continued to progress, I'd have the opportunity

to get a scholarship so I could go to college and further my education," Howard said. "That was really big, really important for my dad and I."

It wouldn't be easy, though. To go to St. Joseph, Howard was required to find his way clear across town each day. "I learned the value of sacrifice," he said. "I had to wake up at 5:30 every morning to go to St. Joe's, and I had to cut some friends loose; I just didn't have time to hang out anymore. In order to succeed, you have to sacrifice and you also need a plan."

His parents weren't worried. They knew how driven Desmond was to succeed. "Even if Desmond had two broken legs, he could still climb to the mountain top," his mother said.

Basketball was supposed to be what would take Desmond to greatness, but at St. Joe's, it quickly became apparent that it wasn't his only option. "Desmond was a good basketball player," J.D. Howard told The Associated Press. "That's why he wanted to go to St. Joseph's. But after he scored five touchdowns in his first varsity football game, I said, 'Maybe we better rethink this thing.' "

DESMOND'S HIGH SCHOOL HIGHLIGHTS

The 5-foot-10, 160-pound senior running back rushed for 1,650 yards on 247 carries for St. Joseph and was named to the Cleveland Plain-Dealer's All-Scholastic Team. A first-team Division I All-Ohio selection, he scored 18 touchdowns, and also played safety on defense, setting a Vikings' school record with 10 interceptions.

On Sept. 5, 1986, Howard, then a junior, scored five touchdowns in his first varsity game, leading St. Joe's over Euclid, 41-28.

Sports

SATURDAY, SEPTEMBER 6, 1986   SECTION B

Celebration
Des Howard (27) was the star last ni___ ___ St. Joseph downed Euclid, 41-28. **Story on Page 3.**

Chris Russell/News-Herald

"Desmond's work-ethic was very high. I can recall when he came to campus — they always said to dress for the career that you want to have — Desmond would go to class in a shirt and tie and sport coat, carry a briefcase and he was just setting a path for himself. He always applied himself to his schoolwork and got very good grades. He was just that type of person. It wasn't easy to do what he did, especially with all of the distractions that young athletes are faced with on a daily basis. But Desmond was the kind of guy that wasn't going to let all of the distractions bring him down or pull him the wrong way."

OTIS WILLIAMS
Michigan
Strong Safety, 1987-91

Academics were equally as important as athletics

While Desmond Howard's athletic accomplishments as a young boy were reaching astonishing levels, his parents made sure that his academics didn't suffer as a consequence.

His parents – J.D. and Hattie – made sure that the four boys – Jonathan, Chad, Desmond and Jermaine – put as much effort into their homework as they did into the extracurricular activities that they all enjoyed.

However, the Howards became alarmed by the number of times that Desmond was sent home from Gracemount Elementary School. His rambunctious behavior often resulted in fights with classmates and other unacceptable outbursts. But it wasn't just at school either. He duked it out on street corners and in the shopping mall; he exhibited a typical adolescent behavior. "I was very outgoing. A friendly and competitive young man, but if confronted I never backed down from a fight," Desmond said.

"He was in so many fights in school that he kept getting sent home," recalled Desmond's younger brother, Jermaine. "Mom and J.D. were the driving force to get Desmond to go to Whitney Young, which was a magnet school at the time."

While some Gracemount officials were quick to diagnose their son as having Attention Deficit Disorder (ADD), Hattie wasn't buying their evaluation of Desmond.

"If there was something wrong with Desmond, I wanted to know," Hattie said. "But I wasn't going to let him get lost in the system. If there was truly something wrong, why hide from it? Let's get him the help that he needs."

After urging the school district to test their son, the Howards were relieved to learn that Desmond wasn't ADD after all. Instead, he was diagnosed as being gifted. It was determined that his classroom tantrums were the results of him not having enough work to do.

"He flew off the charts on the test," Jermaine said. "The problem was that he was frustrated because he was bored. He was finishing his work before the other kids and then he'd start talking in class and try to find something to do."

Even after Desmond changed schools, his father was determined not to allow his son to miss out on the single-most valuable thing that had escaped him as a young child. And that was an opportunity.

"I didn't have that path, and Desmond doesn't know this and my other sons don't know this either," J.D. said. "When I was about six or seven-years-old, I caught double pneumonia, and I was in the Charity Hospital down on Central (Ave.). The doctor told my

mother and father, 'Well, he won't make it through the night.' We had just come up from the South and I wasn't dressing right for the wintertime. They couldn't believe that I came around because they expected that by morning I'd be gone.

"When I got home, I spent most of the time in bed trying to get better, so I missed a lot of school because I was too weak. Elementary school and the rest of it bypassed me. And I never really caught up with it. I never told the boys that because I didn't want them to think I was using that as an excuse for me getting down on them about their schoolwork."

But J.D.'s boyhood experience was enough to help him and Hattie motivate their boys to buckle down when it came to academics.

"At our house we had a big table and when they came home from school, it wasn't about taking a break. It wasn't about watching TV. It was about sitting there and getting your homework done," J.D. said. "You get your homework done then you can go outside and talk to your friends for a minute, then come in, get cleaned up and get ready to eat. That's the way it was in our house, because I didn't get it. But I made sure that they got it."

The preaching paid off, and by the time Desmond reached Ann Arbor it was his work ethic in the classrooms of Whitney Young and St. Joseph High School that were as impressive as anything he did on the hardwood or gridiron.

When Marc Jacobson arrived on the Ann Arbor campus at the same time as Desmond, the two struck up a conversation during freshmen orientation. Immediately the two formed a friendship, and it wasn't long before Jacobson got to see Desmond's scholarly side.

"Desmond was very, very studious and all about the presentation," said Jacobson, a student manager on UM's football team. "The first day of class he's dressed up. He's got a suit and tie on, and he's got a briefcase. And he looks at me in jeans and a T-shirt and says, 'Where do you think you're going?' He said, 'Listen, this is our first day of college. We have to make a good presentation. The way you dress is the way you feel.' And that's how it all started, I mean, he started from that day. He saw the opportunity that was given to him through the sports world, but he appreciated it more then anybody will ever know."

2 TRANSITION GAME

Howard takes time to

catch on as a receiver

As a high school senior, Desmond Howard was facing the most difficult decision of his life — would it be Michigan, Ohio State or somewhere else?

Wearing No. 26, Howard was selected to play for the North team in the annual Ohio All-Star Classic at Massillon's Tiger Stadium in 1988.

A young man from Ohio, many expected him to lean toward the Buckeyes, but ultimately, when he weighed all the options, Michigan was his champion.

"The tradition of Michigan played a big role in my decision," Howard said. "The funny thing is, I didn't realize it at the time. But my dad did. As a kid, you don't see the big picture, but there are certain things that stay in the back of your mind. And it's not until you reflect on those moments later on in life that you realize what wasn't clear in your younger years.

"My dad had the clarity. He had the wisdom."

It didn't hurt the Wolverines that they had an entrenched legend in charge of the program in the form of coach Bo Schembechler, while Ohio State was in the process of making a coaching change from Earle Bruce to John Cooper.

"I wouldn't say that's why Michigan won," Howard said. "I

would just say that Ohio State was taken off the table because of that. I liked both schools, but truth be told, I always liked Michigan more, yet the uncertainty at head coach made Ohio State no longer an option.

"At the time I was being recruited, Ohio State had just fired Earle Bruce and was bringing in John Cooper. I didn't want to be part of a rebuilding program. I wanted to be part of a program that was already established, so I could go to the Rose Bowl."

That Elvis Grbac of Willoughby, Ohio, Howard's high school quarterback at Cleveland St. Joseph, had also chosen the Wolverines as his school, was another factor contributing to his decision. Grbac didn't start until his senior season, and the Vikings built their run-oriented offense around pitches from Grbac to Howard. "Elvis used to throw Desmond a pass every second or third game," Schembechler told The Associated Press in 1989.

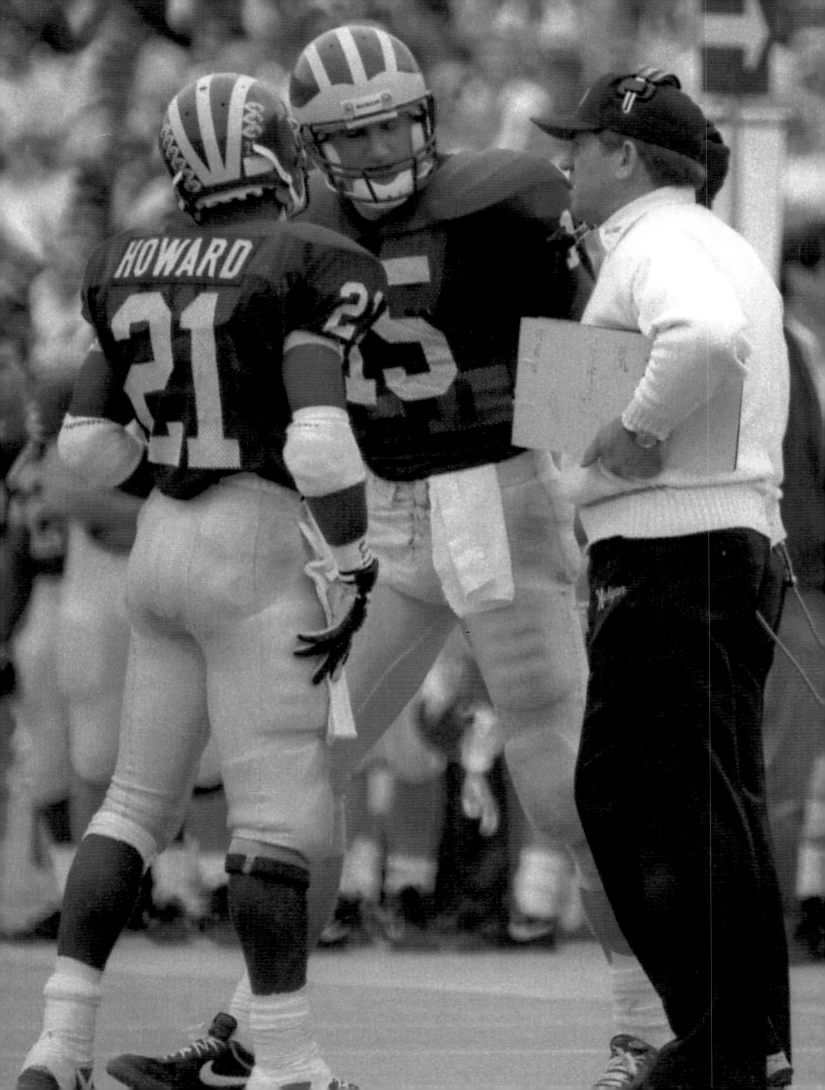

"*He had the talent, definitely. But when he got moved up to the bantamweight team, we were loaded. When Desmond played on the peewee team he was a running back for them. But that second year with us I called him in and told him, 'We're going to move you out to wide out.' He didn't take kindly to that. He didn't take kindly at all to that. But he went to wide out, begrudgedly. We were a running team with the wishbone and veer attack. Teams would shut our running game down. So we would go air, and Desmond was one we threw it to ... a lot. He was going to be one of our featured backs, but we had other guys who got bigger and Desmond didn't really grow that much. We liked to pound the ball, but Desmond was much more dangerous when you put him in space. We just let him do his thing.*"

BRUCE WALKER
St. Tim's Saints, Cleveland Municipal League Coach, 1978-2003

That would all change at Michigan. Howard wasn't going to play tailback. The Wolverines penciled him in as a flanker.

"In high school, I was a tailback," said Howard, who ran for 1,650 yards in his senior season. "They handed me the ball 25-30 times a game. I ran the ball a lot. I think I caught one pass for a touchdown my whole high school career. I was also a defensive back. In my younger years I played corner, but as I got older, I played safety because that was the last line of defense."

Now, the Wolverines were asking Howard to outwit corners and safeties, running routes to elude them without the ball in his hands.

"Switching to wide receiver, it's a different skill set," Howard said. "As a tailback, everything is in front of you. As a wide receiver, you have to turn your back to the defense to catch the ball, and then turn around. You've got to know how to run a route, read coverages, know adjustments and see the same thing as the quarterback. And at Michigan, you had to block. And I mean really, really block. It was as important as anything else you did."

The transition from runner to receiver was not what you would call fluid for Howard. "No, it wasn't smooth at all," he said. "It was rough because of the different skill set that you have to use. When I played municipal football in Cleveland, I played wide receiver for maybe one or two years when I was younger. But I was always a tailback after that. Always a tailback."

"We used to fish a lot with J.D. and his brother, our uncle Ernie. We would go fishing at Mosquito Lake and Old Lady Creek for perch, big mouth bass. I remember one time we went out real late at night and we didn't have any fishing licenses. The park supervisor came riding up on us quick, and they handed us the fishing rods real quick, so we were excused because we were kids and didn't need fishing licenses yet. We cracked up about that. ... One day we caught 105 fish. That was our biggest catch ever. We had gone out to this lake and rented a little boat that you had to row. Desmond was too little to row, so Jonathan and me rowed the boat out far enough, and started fishing. We were there almost 10 hours. Once we got home, J.D. was teaching us how to clean the fish, but we weren't getting it 100 percent, so he would always have to go over them again."

CHAD JONES (FAR LEFT)
Desmond's Older Brother

The night after scoring four TDs for St. Joe's, Desmond (R) dedicated his performance to oldest brother, Jonathan (L), who was home on leave from the Air Force. Jermaine is in the middle.

"Desmond loved to play Atari Defender. We had an arcade up our street, and every neighborhood has its bully when you're growing up. There was this bigger kid, who had to be 3-4 years older than Desmond. He would mess with Desmond when he was playing that game; he'd shove Desmond off the game, and then shove him again. Desmond came home and got my oldest brother, Jonathan, and went back to the arcade with him and pointed the kid out to him. ... That kid never messed with Desmond and that game ever again. Even to this day, Jonathan is Desmond's closest bodyguard."

JERMAINE HOWARD
Desmond's younger brother

Desmond and his Super Bowl MVP award – a 1997 F-150 Ford Lariat 4x4 – that he gave to his oldest brother, Jonathan (R).

In fact, Howard modeled his game after the 1976 Heisman Trophy winner at the University of Pittsburgh, and later an NFL star for the Dallas Cowboys. "Tony Dorsett was my guy," Howard explained. "I would pretend I was Dorsett every time we played football."

Instead, the Wolverines wanted him to play like another Tony who was a Cowboys star of that era, Tony Hill, a tenacious blocker, who eventually became a top-notch receiver.

"It was a bumpy road," Howard said. "Cam Cameron, who was our wide receivers coach, and I didn't see eye to eye in the beginning. So it's safe to say it wasn't a smooth transition from the onset.

"However, the issue I had with Cam was with blocking, and once I changed my attitude about that, and other things without the ball in my hands, then that's when the change took place."

Eventually, Howard came around to see the light. He sought Harden, the school's director of athletic counseling, and Dr. Harry Edwards, the noted sports sociologist.

"I think I knew it was going to work after I had several conversations to help me understand mentally what I was going through with a gentleman at Michigan named Greg Harden," Howard said. "Without Greg Harden, I don't know if I would have gone on to win the Heisman Trophy. I also had conversations with Dr. Harry Edwards. I sought him out.

"I would say the most important thing that I got out of those conversations, which was consistent with both, was that I ended up – for various reasons – changing my attitude. When you change your attitude, you can change your game. That's the best sell."

As he'd come to understand as a youngster growing up in Cleveland, the hard way is often the best way, if success is the ultimate goal at the end of the journey.

"Now his height hurt him at times, compared to the big receivers. But he could lay out. He would kick it into another gear and lay out, like he did against Notre Dame. But he was hard to play 1-on-1 because he could start in on you and if you didn't go when he was running the slant he was back in your hip pocket. And he knew how much time that he could take. Some guys you see down in the corner of the end zone and all of a sudden the throw is late and goes out-of-bounds. The receiver runs out there too fast. They have to start in and you've got to buy space, bringing the corner in with you and then make it a foot race to the corner of the end zone. Desmond knew exactly how to do that! You talk about a guy who could get away from you, Desmond could do that in a hurry."

GARY MOELLER
Michigan
Assistant Coach, 1969-76, 1980-89; Head Coach, 1990-94

"*Desmond had this car that we would borrow. We drove that car around and treated him as a rookie from time to time. He was younger than us and though he had access to this car, we were going to use it to our discretion. We were just happy to have the transportation when he came along. ... He was a great athlete; kind of quiet in his younger years, but of course he blossomed in his later years. He just went about his business as a student-athlete. We knew he had skills, but it wasn't really shown until his junior year.*"

CHRIS CALLOWAY
Michigan
Wide Receiver, 1986-89

"When we got on campus, and everybody obviously understood and appreciated what the Fab Five was and what we brought to the table, but we had a Super Six. I used to joke with Desmond that he was the most famous person on campus. I remember the joy that I got when he put up that Heisman pose against Ohio State and the diving touchdown on fourth and one against Notre Dame. I'm a huge football fan and a huge Desmond Howard fan. So I remember being on campus when we were peers, I definitely wore his jersey.

"He was a terrific player; a game-changer. He was one of the first hybrid players in college sports. A player like a Deion Sanders, a Rocket Ismail, Tim Brown, Charles Woodson, these are players that were hybrids. They didn't play one position; they played multiple positions to change the game. Des played in the slot, Des played receiver, Des played on special teams. He made big catches, he made timely plays. I never played football, because I didn't want to get hit. But will tell you that I know more football than I do basketball, and Desmond was a special player."

JALEN ROSE
Michigan Basketball
Guard 1991-94: All-America, 1994

"If you trace my history, education has always been important," Howard said. "The decision to go to a school like Michigan, the decision to go to a school like St. Joe's, people don't understand that those weren't decisions that just happened. I didn't just go to my neighborhood high school, just because all my friends went to the neighborhood high school. Even as far back as my childhood playing muni-league football, I went a long way from home to play. I can show it to you on a Google map. I went across town to a team that I felt was better and where I felt I would get better coaching. I used to ride my bike all the way across town.

"I could have easily walked to practice for the football team in my neighborhood where my friends played. I could have walked to practice with my friends, like most kids do. But instead, I got on my bike, rode across town and ended up competing against my friends on another football team. That may give you a glimpse into my psychological makeup at an early age."

Howard was driven to achieve and was willing to make the necessary sacrifices along the way.

"My dad will tell you," he said. "Anybody who knows Cleveland, if you look at where I lived, and you look at where I went to high school, that was a sacrifice. I had almost a two-hour bus ride on a city bus every morning to get to school. There was a much easier route, but I didn't take that easier route. I took the route that I thought would give me the best coaching, that would let me participate and compete against the best competition. We played the best teams in the state of Ohio. And at the same time, give me the best education to prepare me for college. I'm getting up and catching a bus at 6:15 in the morning to get to school by 8:15. That's every morning."

Howard has never been one to shy away from a commitment. And once he committed himself to the receiver position, the sky would be his limit.

"Desmond and I were roommates in orientation, and we just hit it off immediately. And his friend from St. Joe's in Cleveland, Eric Riley, was a basketball player, and we just ended up paling around. I remember one time the three of us went out to explore the campus on our own and we missed some orientation things because we got lost for two hours in the middle of nowhere by foot. Those three days obviously started the relationship that is now 23 years and going. Now he's an uncle to my children and I'm an uncle to his children. He certainly has been one of the best friends that you could ever have. He's all about family and friends."

MARC JACOBSON (Below Right)
Desmond's Friend and College Roommate
Michigan, Football Manager, 1988-91

The recruiting process that came full-circle for Howard

As Desmond Howard neared the end of his junior football season at Cleveland St. Joseph, recruitment letters from prominent collegiate football programs from all across the country streamed in by the dozens.

While Michigan and Ohio State were believed to be front-runners for Howard's college loyalty, there were other programs vying for his football services. Besides Ann Arbor, Howard made official campus visits to Georgia Tech, Michigan State, Syracuse and Purdue.

Though Michigan eventually won the Desmond Howard sweepstakes, J.D. Howard said his son was also intrigued by what he heard from coaches at the United States Military Academy at West Point. No doubt, Desmond's work ethic and dedication, coupled with his academic achievements and athletic endeavors, made him an ideal cadet candidate.

There was no way to know then, but Howard's football career would travel full-circle when in his waning NFL seasons he was reunited with the man who tried like crazy to persuade him to leave Big Ten country.

Georgia Tech defensive backs coach Chuck Priefer, who grew up in Parma, Ohio – and later coached high school football there – liked what he saw in young Desmond. But Priefer saw something that most coaches didn't see in Howard.

"People don't realize that he was a tough kid, and I really thought that he could be a defensive back, I really did," said Priefer, who later became Desmond's special teams coach with the Detroit Lions.

Part of Priefer's recruiting assessment was based on a particular goal line hit that Howard delivered during a state playoff game at the Rubber Bowl in Akron.

"He just blew that kid up," recalled Priefer.

John Storey, who was Desmond's defensive backs coach at St. Joe's, agreed with Priefer's recollection of the hit on Youngstown Boardman fullback Jason Marucci, a 205-pounder, who later played at Miami (Fla.).

"We played an attack defense with everybody pretty much up on the line of scrimmage, manned up, and Desmond was playing free," Storey said. "They were a Wing-T team and Marucci was going to come off-tackle. Des kind of read the play and dove over the line of scrimmage, hitting Marucci right in the shoulder-neck area and just staggered the guy."

"That just tells of Des's personality; he just took his body – all 150 pounds of it – and hurled himself over the top of the pile and hit this guy. Of all the plays that I've been a part of in high school and college, that's the play that I'll always remember."

Nearly 25 years later, that goal-line play is why Priefer says he and his boss, Yellow Jackets head coach Bobby Ross, stayed in contact with Howard for as long as they did.

"Desmond wasn't Michigan's highest recruited guy, and they never thought he would become what he became," Priefer said. "Back in those days, the head coach had to be the one to make the offer to the kids. I asked Desmond if he had talked to Bo. And he hadn't. He told me that someone had died and that Bo was at a funeral."

It was then, just a few days away from National Signing Day that Priefer said he saw a glimmer of hope, which might place a star recruit in the Yellow Jackets' lap.

"I told Desmond, 'If you don't hear from Coach Schembechler or things change, you make sure to call me and I'll drive up there.'" Priefer said. "I figured I'd call Mo thinking that maybe Michigan had backed off the kid. I didn't know what they were thinking because he was 165 or 170 pounds.

"So I called Gary, who I've known since I was a high school coach and he used to recruit us for Michigan. This is a true story: he says, 'Well Chuck, Bo is probably going to take him,' and he says, 'What do you think, is he good enough?' And I said, 'Mo, we've been recruiting this kid – the both of us – for a year and a half, and I guarantee he's good enough. You know he's good enough.'"

The old coaching buddies still laugh about that story.

"We had this play that was designed for goal line and short yardage situations. The linemen would submarine the defensive linemen. It was like a power-I set with the flanker behind the guard. Those two guys would go in there and I used to come in and jump over the top. Every time we used that play we always got a first down.

"Now if you can picture someone trying to block a field goal where the defensive backs come from the back and jumps up and over; that's exactly what Desmond did. I mean, he was almost inverted with his head down and his legs straight up in the air, and we came helmet to helmet. As I was about to jump up, he came down on my head. Yeah, I remember that one. There wasn't a pain factor, but it was just the shock of that play not working because it had worked every time that year. ... And there was nobody that we played that was that athletic to get that high and jump over like he did."

JASON MARUCCI (41)
Youngstown Boardman
Fullback, 1987-88

DESMOND HOWARD

3 AMAZING IN MAIZE AND BLUE

Assuming a starring role,

Howard accomplishes things

not previously achieved by

a Wolverines player

After sitting out the 1988 season as a redshirt freshman and learning the ins and outs of the receiver position, Howard was ready to take on a larger role at Michigan during the 1989 campaign.

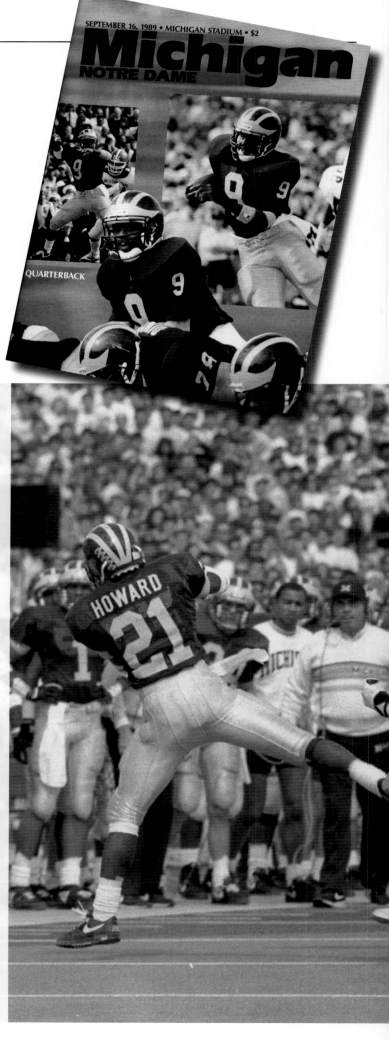

SEPTEMBER 16, 1989 • MICHIGAN STADIUM • $2

Michigan
NOTRE DAME

QUARTERBACK

HOWARD
21

Howard's versatility was evident prior to the 1989 season, when he joined with football teammates Tripp Welborne, Lance Dottin, Vada Murray and Derrick Walker to win the Michigan intramural basketball championship. "I think Michigan basically came after me as an athlete who could probably fill spots at any of the three positions," said Howard, who worked as a kick and punt return man and receiver.

Michigan coach Bo Schembechler saw Howard fitting in as one of his messenger receivers in a rotation with starters Greg McMurtry and Chris Calloway. "He's a little guy with real good speed," Schembechler told The Michigan Daily of Howard. "He's a young guy with a lot of talent who is capable of making the big play, but he lacks experience."

Howard caught nine balls that season for 136 yards, a 15.1 yards-per-catch average and two touchdowns as Michigan went 10-2 and won the Big Ten title. Howard's first TD as a Wolverine came in a 42-27 rout of Purdue, snaring an eight-yard pass from quarterback Michael Taylor.

His first score for Michigan would also be his last touchdown pass received from Taylor. During a 49-15 drubbing of Minnesota, Howard got on the other end of a 19-yard scoring pass from Elvis Grbac, and a beautiful relationship was reborn.

Grbac was Howard's quarterback in high school at Cleveland St. Joseph, though in those days, he turned and handed the ball to Howard, who worked in the backfield as a tailback. "We lived in different parts of town," Grbac recalled. "We weren't that close socially, but we had this friendship right from the start because of sports."

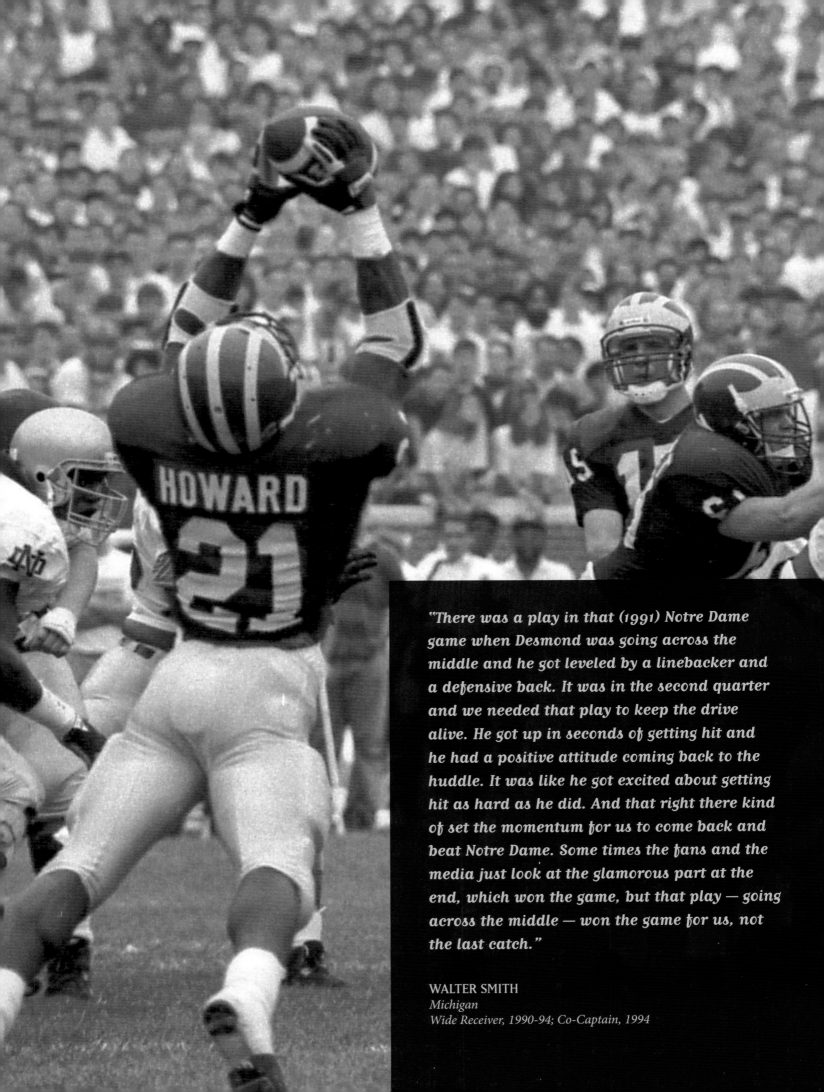

"There was a play in that (1991) Notre Dame game when Desmond was going across the middle and he got leveled by a linebacker and a defensive back. It was in the second quarter and we needed that play to keep the drive alive. He got up in seconds of getting hit and he had a positive attitude coming back to the huddle. It was like he got excited about getting hit as hard as he did. And that right there kind of set the momentum for us to come back and beat Notre Dame. Some times the fans and the media just look at the glamorous part at the end, which won the game, but that play — going across the middle — won the game for us, not the last catch."

WALTER SMITH
Michigan
Wide Receiver, 1990-94; Co-Captain, 1994

"*Magical things seem to happen for him. But there's a lot of effort that goes into that. There are a couple of times when he stood out, and they are memorable. I just don't remember too many times where he attempted something and he wasn't able to do. That's what makes the two-point conversion attempt against Michigan State in 1990 that memorable. Yeah, he got tackled; that was kind of expected, because you knew that he was going to juke the guy. And that was the guy's only chance of stopping him. The only amazing part was that Desmond didn't catch the ball.*"

J.D. CARLSON
Michigan
Place-Kicker, 1988-91; All-Big Ten, 1989-91

Between them, they would hook up for 31 TD passes at Michigan, an NCAA record, proving that a little knowledge can go a long way. "If nothing else, it gave us the confidence in each other," said Howard, of his relationship with Grbac. "We had a familiarity. We knew each other's competitive level and competitive spirit.

"As opposed to going out there and playing with some quarterback from Eugene, Oregon, or Iowa, or from someplace where I didn't know the guy and you've kind of got to feel him out, learn what his work ethic is like, see if he shows up on game day. I didn't have to worry about that with Elvis, and Elvis didn't have to worry about that with me. He knew come game time, 'I saw this kid in high school. I know he's going to be there. I don't care what position you're going to put him in, come game time, he's going to do what he has to do.' And vice-versa."

"He and Chris Calloway became very close friends when Chris was a senior, and I was in my fifth year. When we would go on road trips, Desmond was a freshman and didn't travel, so he would stay at our place on Brown Street when we were out of town. We wouldn't get back until late Saturday night after a game and lo and behold, Desmond was there as inquisitive as ever. He took leadership the right way and learned from the guys ahead of him. He was like a sponge, just soaked up all of the knowledge. He was a kid that did everything the right way."

DERRICK WALKER
Michigan
Tight End, 1985-89; Co-Captain, All-Big Ten, 1989

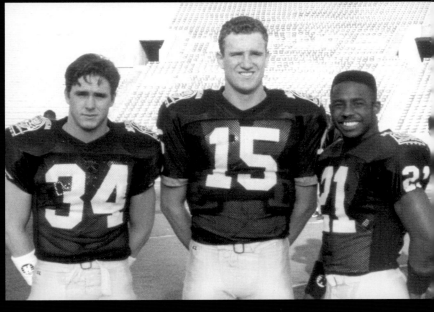

While the Wolverines readied for the 1990 season, there was optimism, even though starting receivers Calloway and McMurtry had both graduated and been drafted by NFL teams. The optimism was created by the two kids stepping into those starting roles: Howard and Derrick Alexander, who like Howard, was a converted running back.

"They are better than I thought," new UM head coach Gary Moeller – who had been promoted when the legendary Schembechler retired following the 1989 season – told The Daily Reporter. "Potentially, they can be better than Calloway and McMurtry. They have better running ability."

Howard moved over from flanker to split end and started all 12 games. "We should accomplish a lot together," Howard predicted of his partnership with Alexander.

Off the field, Howard, a communications major, carried an impressive 3.0 grade-point average, and he was also turning heads on the field. "Desmond has really impressed the coaches this spring," Wolverines tight end Derrick Walker told The Michigan Daily. "Howard will be a big plus to us this fall."

It didn't take long for Howard to serve notice that he would live up to that billing. In a season-opening 28-24 loss at Notre Dame, he caught touchdown passes of 25 and 44 yards from Grbac, but was devastated when the Wolverines let a 24-14 lead disappear. "I would have given those two touchdowns up to win the Notre Dame game, quick," Howard said.

During that game, Howard had six catches for 136 yards, and Jon Vaughn rushed for 201 yards. It marked the first time the Wolverines had a 100-yard receiver and 200-yard rusher in the same game since 1968 against Duke, when Ron Johnson (RIGHT) ran for 205 yards and Jerry Imsland had 103 yards in receptions during a 31-10 victory over the Blue Devils.

Howard snared three more scoring passes over the next three games, all of them Michigan victories, then ran a kickoff back 95 yards against Michigan State, a game in which he was front and center in the most controversial play of the 1990 NCAA football season.

Trailing 28-21 to the Spartans, Grbac hit Alexander on a seven-yard TD pass with six seconds to play. Opting to go for two points and the win, Moeller called a pass play to Howard in the back of the end zone. Television replays showed that Howard was held and then tripped by Michigan State defensive back Eddie Brown before the pass arrived, and even though the ball slid through Howard's grasp as he fell, pass interference was not called.

Regardless, Moeller was effusive in his praise of Howard. "He worked his rear end off this summer in spring ball, summer ball, two-a-day practices," Moeller told The Michigan Daily of his redshirt sophomore receiver. "He worked hard and he did what he was told to do.

"He's showed some good quickness, some good speed. He's the kind of guy that likes the football. You can tell that as soon as he catches it, he goes right back to that old running back."

After falling to 3-3 following a loss to Iowa, Michigan rallied to win its last six games, including a 35-3 rout of Mississippi in the Gator Bowl. Howard finished the season with 63 catches for 1,025

The 46th
Annual

MAZDA GATOR BOWL

Michigan vs. Mississippi
January 1, 1991
Jacksonville, Florida
Official Souvenir Program $5

DESMOND HOWARD
FUN FACTS

Awards won by Desmond Howard at Michigan

1991
NATIONAL
- **Heisman Trophy**
- **Walter Camp Award**
  Coaches' player of the year
- **Maxwell Award**
  Maxwell Football Club's top player
- **All-American Selection**
- **Chic Harley Award**
  Touchdown Club of Columbus Player of the Year
- **Paul Warfield Trophy**
  Top wide receiver
- **Sporting News Player of the Year**
- **UPI Player of the Year**

BIG TEN CONFERENCE
- **Most Valuable Player**
- **Athlete of the Year**
- **Offensive Player of the Year**
- **All-Conference Selection**

MICHIGAN
- **Most Valuable Player**
- **Meyer Morton Award**
  'M' Club of Chicago's top spring football pla

1990
NATIONAL
- **All-American Selection**

BIG TEN CONFERENCE
- **All-Conference Selection**

"It couldn't have been more than two weeks into camp. It was our freshman year. Without going into grizzly details, Desmond ended up in a fight with Brian Wallace, a 300-pound lineman. Desmond was not backing down a bit. Damn, what was he, 175-pounds, soaking wet? I just remember Desmond going after this guy with no backup. But I remember thinking, 'That kid has a lot of heart and he's not worried about getting hurt.'

"The thing about that 1991 season, you would think that we would have stuffed it up somebody on a fourth-and-one or a third-down conversion. We had a great line that year, but we were throwing to Desmond on fourth-and-short, and not just the Notre Dame game. Every week, he was sliding into the band or making a crazy catch. And everybody knew he was going to do it. I can't remember a receiver in college dominating the way he did ... ever.

"But like that fight he got into with the 300-pounder, he never thought about the consequences of throwing his body around the way he did. He doesn't get credit for the way Cam Cameron had them blocking back in those days. ... Desmond was a kick-ass blocker and he didn't get credit for that, not as if that wins you a Heisman. But Desmond didn't take plays off. "

STEVE EVERITT
Michigan
Offensive Guard/Center, 1988-92; All-Big Ten, 1992

yards, a 16.3 yards-per-catch average and 11 touchdowns. His 29.6 average led the nation's kick returners. "You've got to give him all the attention you possibly can," Ohio State coach John Cooper said.

Howard ran the 40-yard dash in 4.3 seconds. His high-flying, depth-defying, acrobatic catches alone were worth the price of admission to the Big House. His explosiveness added a new dimension to the Michigan offense, earning him second team All-Big Ten status and a return specialist spot on the All-American team in 1990.

"He wasn't the biggest guy, but he was so quick and elusive and he had great hands," recalled former Michigan head coach Lloyd Carr, who was an assistant under both Schembechler and Moeller during Howard's time with the Wolverines.

"He was very popular with his teammates, because he really knew how to handle all the attention that was coming his way and not become big-headed, or let it be a distraction to the team. He was friendly and outgoing and wanted to just be one of the guys on the team.

"It was always about the team first with Desmond."

Those traits came naturally to Howard. "I'm a pretty jovial type of guy," he said. "I like to keep the atmosphere in a happy mood. I think the coaches may have worried about that sometimes when there was a game and I was not as intense as a lot of the other people. Because I'm a jovial person, I could sit and tell jokes until we went on the field."

The loyalty of his character and the team-first attitude was only reinforced during Howard's time with the Wolverines.

"Michigan's all about team, team, team," Howard recalled. "And that was ingrained in us. That was something that was drilled hard into us. It wasn't about any individualism at all. It was always about team.

"I never wanted to do anything to disrespect that. That was big. That was one of the reasons that I believe, and I think we all believed, that we were so successful. We were very unselfish and it was all about the team. What we had to do to win, we would sacrifice to a man to do that. I never wanted to disrupt that."

The only thing Howard ever disrupted was the opposition's plan to contain him.

Blocking became part of Howard's repertoire

As a three-sports star in high school, Desmond Howard muddled through a somewhat rough freshman football season at Michigan.

Not knowing if he would be a tailback, cornerback or wide receiver, the early days in Ann Arbor weren't so simple for Howard, who as a prep senior had scored 18 touchdowns and set a new single-season school record with 10 interceptions at Cleveland St. Joseph.

By his own admission, Howard was becoming a rebellious student-athlete.

As playing time did not increase much in his redshirt sophomore year, Howard sought the advice of an authority figure, a guy in the athletic department that he had heard about. Greg Harden, then in his third year as Michigan's director of athletic counseling, was the figure that became Howard's mentor.

"Desmond came to see me because he wasn't getting any playing time," Harden recalled. "That's why he comes talk to me in the first place; he's frustrated. But like all recruits we promised him the world and you find out that you actually have to work for the world."

The work wasn't so bothersome to Howard; it was the rigors of blocking. But as Harden said, if you're going to play receiver on a predominantly run-heavy offense, then you better learn to block.

"I told him that I was going to do some research on why he wasn't getting the playing time," Harden said. "I told him, 'I'm going to find out what the rap is on you son.' Well, I came back and it wasn't all positive.

"Despite the fact that he managed his ego well, he certainly had one. But without it you can't be that good. He was pretty convinced that he should just start. But what he didn't factor in was that a wide receiver at Michigan is a fierce, possessed blocking machine, something that wasn't in his make-up at the time."

Howard accepted Harden's analysis and became even more driven to succeed. And he allowed his new mentor to become the engineer who would design the highway that Howard eventually travelled to New York City where he collected his Heisman Trophy in runaway fashion.

With the path created, Howard had to work on being a consistently reliable blocker. But to do so, he had to buy into his new mentor's methods.

"I came back to him and said, 'OK, you don't block, you don't like to block,'" Harden said. "'Why don't you try this? At least once every week piss-off the defensive coordinator and bust somebody's ass.'

"Well, not only did he do it, he got good at it, because he is a fairly aggressive lad. He soon found a passion for knocking people on their butts, which is the only way you're going to get into a program that's built off the run. If you want to get on the field, you have to block for the running back. Period. You say you're a great receiver. Who cares? If you can't block, we'll never know."

Michigan coaches soon liked what they saw in Howard, especially when he blocked a Notre Dame cornerback to the ground – not once, not twice, but three times – on the same play. Four plays later, Howard took a reverse hand-off from Ricky Powers, broke free from Irish cornerback Rod Smith, and sprinted 29-yards for the touchdown.

"Desmond is the only (receiver) that we had to get a triple-knockdown," former UM quarterbacks and receivers coach Cam Cameron said. "It's knocking a guy off his feet three times in the same play. And I remember him getting (Tom Carter) three times. ... That's the kind of blocker he was."

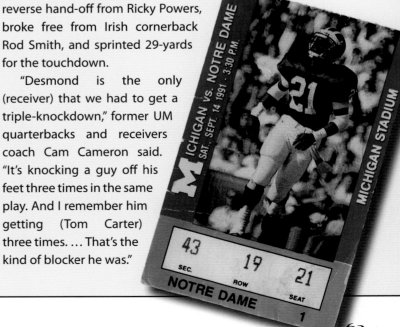

4 STRIKING THE POSE

Howard runs away with

the Heisman Trophy

Fresh off a season-opening four-touchdown performance during a 35-13 victory over Boston College, the question was posed to Desmond Howard.

What did he think of his chances of winning the Heisman Trophy?

Truth be told, he didn't think about those chances at all. Howard reasoned that if Anthony Carter, Michigan's all-time receiving leader, hadn't gotten any love from the voters, then why would he garner their attention?

Entering the season, Houston quarterback David Klingler and Penn State quarterback Tony Sacca garnered the most notice when the Heisman contenders were listed. Brigham Young quarterback Ty Detmer, the 1990 Heisman winner, and

Florida State QB Casey Weldon were also in the running, but they would prove to be also-rans behind Howard.

His opening-day performance made Howard just the seventh Michigan player to score four touchdowns in a game and the first since Rob Lytle in 1975. A 93-yard kickoff return in the win also made Howard just the second Michigan player to run back two kicks for scores. He'd returned a kickoff 95 yards for a TD in 1990 against Michigan State.

"I don't know what it is about me, but making the big play when we're behind is what really gets me going," Howard said. "I like doing the spectacular."

"Notre Dame had a pretty good football team that year. But when this guy came around and started doing what he was doing, of course, I hated Desmond. Anybody who was thrashing my Notre Dame boys at that time, you find a way not to like those guys. But when he hit that Heisman pose I thought that was the cockiest thing anybody could ever do. After that I said, 'There's no way I'm voting for him for the Heisman! I don't care what he does!' But certainly, by the time the year ended, he ended up No. 1 on my ballot, that's for sure."

TIM BROWN
Notre Dame
Wide Receiver, 1984-87; Heisman Trophy Winner, 1987

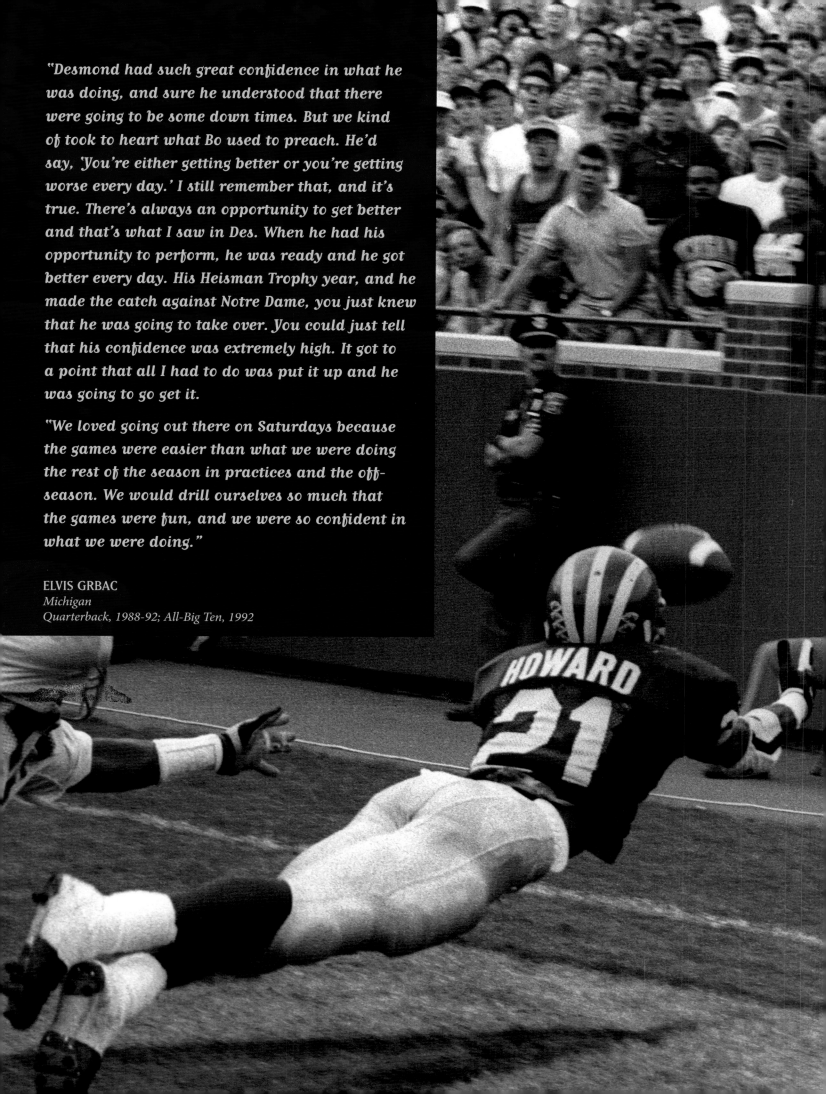

"Desmond had such great confidence in what he was doing, and sure he understood that there were going to be some down times. But we kind of took to heart what Bo used to preach. He'd say, 'You're either getting better or you're getting worse every day.' I still remember that, and it's true. There's always an opportunity to get better and that's what I saw in Des. When he had his opportunity to perform, he was ready and he got better every day. His Heisman Trophy year, and he made the catch against Notre Dame, you just knew that he was going to take over. You could just tell that his confidence was extremely high. It got to a point that all I had to do was put it up and he was going to go get it.

"We loved going out there on Saturdays because the games were easier than what we were doing the rest of the season in practices and the off-season. We would drill ourselves so much that the games were fun, and we were so confident in what we were doing."

ELVIS GRBAC
Michigan
Quarterback, 1988-92; All-Big Ten, 1992

Soon, the nation would take notice. Michigan's next game was against rival Notre Dame, which had dominated the series, winning four straight. In 1991, though, the game belonged to Howard. He made a diving, fingertip catch on fourth down for a 25-yard TD and also scored on a 29-yard reverse as No. 3 Michigan posted a 24-14 victory over the seventh-ranked Fighting Irish.

"I knew it was fourth down and there was no doubt in my mind that I would get the ball," Howard said of his dramatic touchdown grab. "I pulled it in and tucked it away. The crowd roared and it was music to my ears."

Quarterback Elvis Grbac is still amazed by what Howard did that day. "I threw the ball up and it was really incomplete, to tell you the truth," Grbac said. "Then at about the 5-yard line, Des looks up and he goes into another gear and absolutely runs by the corner and there are not too many guys who can do that. That was a catch that just propelled him through the entire season, because now once we got inside the 20-yard line, people were like, 'OK, what's he going to run? Nobody's going to stop him.'"

In defeat, Irish coach Lou Holtz compared Howard's all-around versatility to that of former Notre Dame star Raghib (Rocket) Ismail. "He reminds me so much of Rocket," Holtz said. "He's a lot like Rocket in the things he does."

Suddenly, Howard's name was being bandied about as a Heisman candidate.

"The Notre Dame game was like the New Hampshire primary," ESPN college football analyst Beano Cook told The Associated Press. "Howard took the lead in that game and never gave it up."

Howard noticed the change in his stature after the win over the Irish. "Without a shadow of a doubt, simply because of the power of people's respect for Notre Dame," he said. "The week before, I scored four touchdowns against Boston College and I barely got a blip. On the road, in someone else's backyard, I scored four touchdowns, and it barely got a mention. Then the next week in Ann Arbor, we played Notre Dame and I scored two touchdowns and they're saying, 'Hey, this kid may be pretty good.'"

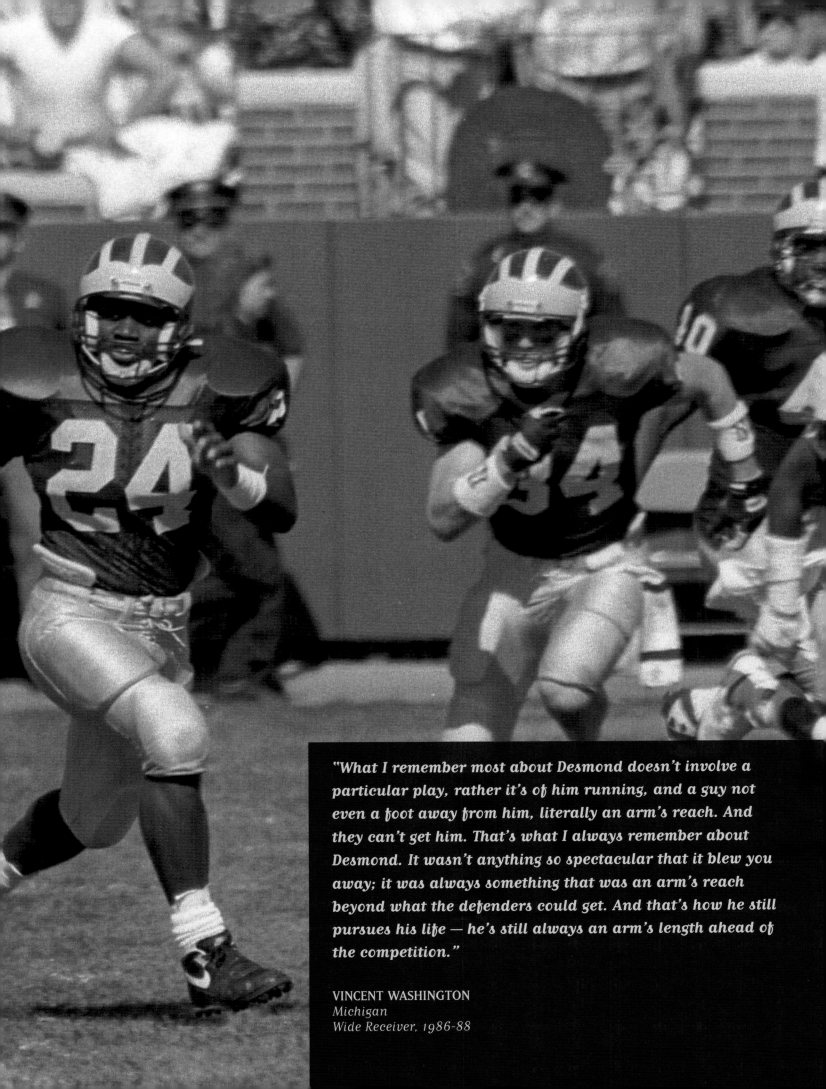

"What I remember most about Desmond doesn't involve a particular play, rather it's of him running, and a guy not even a foot away from him, literally an arm's reach. And they can't get him. That's what I always remember about Desmond. It wasn't anything so spectacular that it blew you away; it was always something that was an arm's reach beyond what the defenders could get. And that's how he still pursues his life — he's still always an arm's length ahead of the competition."

VINCENT WASHINGTON
Michigan
Wide Receiver, 1986-88

The 5-foot-9, 176-pound Howard became the first receiver in Big Ten history to lead the conference in scoring with 90 points in conference games, and he set or tied five NCAA records and 12 single-season Michigan records. Voted MVP of the Wolverines by his teammates, the All-American set standards for most points scored (138) and most touchdowns (23). He was recognized as NCAA player of the year by earning both the Walter Camp Award and the Maxwell Award. Named Big Ten athlete of the year, Howard also captured UPI and AP offensive player of the year honors as well as being named the Dunlop Pro-Am athlete of the year.

There was one award left to win – the Heisman Trophy – and Howard wanted to do something to ensure that people would remember him. His last chance to make such a bold statement would come in the season finale against the Wolverines' archrivals.

"Boston College did not have the same level of respect in football that Notre Dame did. And Tom Coughlin was the head coach at Boston College that year, too. But definitely, that game against Notre Dame put me on the map. It was unbelievable. I scored four against Boston College and it's like, 'Well, that was a nice performance.' But two against Notre Dame and the next thing I know, I'm on the cover of Sports Illustrated."

An unstoppable force throughout the 1991 season, Howard recorded 23 touchdowns during the year, 19 on pass receptions. The latter mark is still the Big Ten record, surpassing the previous mark of 14 set by Michigan's Carter. Howard scored at least two touchdowns in nine of 11 games and set an NCAA record 10 games in a row with at least one TD pass reception. Going back to the 1990 season, his mark of 13 straight games with a touchdown catch is also a Big Ten standard that remains on the books today.

"Desmond had some great stats and some great plays. I mean, that catch in that (1991) Notre Dame game is unbelievable. And then to come back and run that punt back against Ohio State. And don't forget the year before in that Michigan State game when he got interfered with — we thought — and we went for two (points) and should have kicked an extra-point. Well the next year, Desmond came back and I think he caught two passes in that same area for touchdowns. That's how committed of a guy he was; he really wanted to redeem himself."

GARY MOELLER
Michigan
Assistant Coach, 1969-76, 1980-89;
Head Coach, 1990-94

"Being from Ohio, I thought about doing something special, but I didn't know exactly what I was going to do," Howard said. "As the momentum started to build, people started to say things and make suggestions. One person was a teammate of mine who played defensive back named Lance Dottin. I think Lance approached me following the Boston College game, because Lance was from that area, and said, 'Man you're going to be a Heisman candidate, a front runner. You should do something spectacular after you score a touchdown.' I was like, 'No, no. We've got to let this thing play out. We've got the whole season.' But as the season grew, I talked to Lance, again, and he said, 'Man, I'm telling you. You've got to do something in the end zone,' because I was just handing the ball to the ref.

"At the end of the season, it was clear that I was definitely a front runner. I said, 'Hey, if I get in the end zone against Ohio State, being that I was born and raised in Cleveland, Ohio – so this rivalry is pretty special to me – I have to do something significant.' "

Ahead of the Buckeyes, 17-3 late in the first half, Howard's chance finally arrived. He gathered in a punt from Ohio State's Tim Williams, split a pair of tacklers at the 10-yard line, then broke another tackle at the 18. Moving down the Ohio State sideline, he picked up a key block from Dwayne Ware at the 30, and was off to the races.

As he reached the end zone, in perhaps the most famous photo in Michigan football history, a jubilant Howard struck the Heisman Trophy statuette pose before he was bowled over by celebratory teammates.

"I really didn't know what I was going to do," Howard said. "That's what I ended up doing. To be honest with you, I debated it the whole time. I almost didn't do it. I'm talking about when I'm running the punt back. I'm still thinking, 'Do I want to do this, or not?' I didn't know how it was going to be perceived. I was a young kid, trying to do something creative, without getting a penalty."

Howard's 93-yard runback in the 31-3 victory over the Buckeyes broke the school record of 88 yards set by Dave Brown against Colorado in 1974.

"It was during his junior high and high school years that he would come up and spend summers with me in Detroit. At the time I was working at Wayne State University as an assistant basketball coach, and because of my relationship with a lot of the basketball coaches, I would send Desmond and my son to other coaches' camps at Western Michigan and University of Detroit.

"It was funny, when he would go to St. Cecilia's to play, it was a little more than he thought it would be. Back then they had all of the players who came to play. I'll tell you who was there — he didn't play with Desmond, but he impressed Desmond — was Antoine Joubert. That's one of the reasons that helped Desmond lean toward Michigan. For some reason, he just impressed Desmond."

CAL DILWORTH (RIGHT)
Desmond's Uncle

"In my mind, I'm thinking that I'm going to catch him. I would have caught him, but I don't know who pushed me. But they tapped me just enough to knock me off because I had a great angle on him. I'm thinking, 'I'm going to catch him right here on national TV.' Whoever pushed me did a good job, and Desmond walked in. ... There's my claim to fame; I'm the last guy to chase him into the end zone."

SCOTTIE GRAHAM
Ohio State
Running Back, 1988-91; Co-Captain, 1991

"I was very close to the Michigan coaching staff because we did so many Michigan games back in those days. But one of their coaches told me, 'Wait until you see this kid; you're not going to believe it.' The first time I saw him he was bright and as shiny as a new dollar, and quicker than anybody on the field. He was a nice kid from Day 1, and still is.

"But the 'Hello, Heisman' play, which was a punt return, neither one of us had talked about it beforehand. It was an absolutely impromptu moment, and it led to one of the better descriptive quotes that I've heard from anybody when I asked him, 'What's it like running back kicks 80-yards? What do you feel when you've got all those guys out there trying to kill ya?' And he said, 'Man, it's like running through a thunderstorm.' I couldn't have said it better myself, in fact, I wish I had."

KEITH JACKSON
College Football Broadcaster, 1952-2006

MICHIGAN
NOVEMBER 23, 1991   MICHIGAN STADIUM
OHIO STATE $3

DESMOND HOWARD
FUN FACTS

1991 HEISMAN TROPHY VOTING

PLACE	NAME	SCHOOL	CLASS	POS.	1	2	3	TOTAL
1st	Desmond Howard	Michigan	Jr.	WR	640	68	21	2,077
2nd	Casey Weldon	Florida State	Sr.	QB	19	175	96	503
3rd	Ty Detmer	Brigham Young	Sr.	QB	19	129	130	445
4th	Steve Emtman	Washington	Jr.	DT	29	100	70	357
5th	Shane Matthews	Florida	Jr.	QB	11	72	69	246
6th	Vaughn Dunbar	Indiana	Sr.	TB	6	51	53	173
7th	Jeff Blake	East Carolina	Sr.	QB	7	29	35	114
8th	Terrell Buckley	Florida State	Jr.	DB	1	24	51	102
9th	Marshall Faulk	San Diego State	Fr.	RB	0	10	32	52

"*I know that everybody loves that Heisman pose, but we had talked about it, and I think he had mentioned it earlier in that week that he would do that pose. I was the last guy coming back to pick-up the last block; that was my responsibility after I made sure that the punt was secured. But as I came back and saw him part the sea, I turned around, and I got the last block on Scottie Graham to spring him. After I put my hands on Scottie Graham I knew nobody else was going to catch Desmond and I just took off after him just to make sure that I would get into the end zone and into that picture for the Heisman pose. But let it be known that I was not the one who took him to the ground! That was not me.*"

DWAYNE WARE (8)
Michigan
Cornerback, 1988-92

Lapel pin from 1991 Heisman ceremony

His flair for the dramatic even caught Howard's family off guard. "I just thought Desmond was clowning around," his mother Hattie Charles told Knight-Ridder Newspapers. "But I knew all about what the Heisman meant.

"Still, whenever I asked about getting a dress and tuxedos for the banquet, Desmond ignored me. He never ignores me. But the first thing he said after the Ohio State game was, 'Now what was that you were saying about a dress and tuxedo?' And he was laughing.

"He had kept all the pressure inside himself, but then he was a volcano erupting. He had weathered the storm and the pressure."

Still, in the back of his mind, Howard prepared for the worst, noting that Ismail, a player of similar ilk to him, had been passed over for the Heisman the year before. "Just because Rocket didn't win

it when a lot of people thought he would, it made a lot of us cautious," Howard said. "I remember having a conversation with Gary Moeller. He pretty much said, 'You deserve the Heisman. There's no doubt about that. You had a fantastic year, one of those special years that you don't see often. But, we know what happened last year. Everyone was sure that Rocket was going to win it and the kid at BYU (Ty Detmer) won it. Don't be discouraged or disappointed if it doesn't happen. But you earned the Heisman.' So I was always kind of on guard for the letdown, so to speak."

On the day the vote was announced, there was no letdown, only an overwhelming rout. Howard was named the 57th Heisman Award winner by a margin of 1,574 points – the second largest in the history of the award – over Florida State's Casey Weldon. Howard garnered 2,077 points and 640 first place votes. "Desmond deserved it,"

THE BACK STORY

Howard's will knew no boundaries

Desmond Howard's collegiate career will forever be remembered by two plays: The diving touchdown catch against Notre Dame that put him on the Heisman Trophy watch list. And the punt return against Ohio State that guaranteed him the famed bronze statue.

But what most don't realize is the amount of blood, sweat and tears that went into Howard's crowning achievement that came at the end of the 1991 college season.

An undersized player from Cleveland, Howard had the will of a lion, which separated him from the rest of the pack. Still, he knew if he were going to be the best player – not only in the Big Ten – but also in the nation, it would take more than skill and a desire to be great.

From a very young age, Howard was determined to map out his life's journey. He understood that if he were to achieve greatness, whether it was in the classroom or on the football field, he would have to meet certain challenges head-on, and then, push even harder.

And it was that approach, which led Howard to seek guidance at Greg Harden's doorstep. Harden, Michigan's director of athletic counseling, had mentored other UM athletes, and had come highly recommended to Howard.

"Desmond was more deliberate and intentional than any

20-year-old kid that I've ever met in my life," Harden said. "He was deliberate and intentional about creating a space in his head where he would not be the enemy. He would not be the victim of self-defeating attitudes and behaviors."

In the months leading up to the 1991 season, Howard firmly jumped on-board with Harden's tactics, and together the pair created measurable goals for the UM receiver. The first goal was to be the best player at his position, Harden said, followed by the best on the team, then the conference, and ultimately, the nation.

To achieve these goals, Harden told his pupil, "While everyone else is having a good time in the summer, drinking a little beer, partying a little bit, you go out in the middle of the night when the sun goes down after it's been 90-degrees, and you make a commitment to run 10 to 15 extra miles a week.

"You commit to having a cardiovascular system that is going to be far and above what everyone else is doing. So when you come into two-a-days and everybody else is throwing up, you're trying not to be amused, and trying to hide how much it doesn't bother you."

With these words, Howard set off for gridiron glory, and never looked back.

Howard began a workout regimen that was akin a world

champion boxer: jumping rope to help increase quickness and agility, long distance runs for endurance, and punching a speed bag to develop better hand-eye coordination.

"He was awfully trusting because I said, 'This is what you need to do, but don't tell anybody, because you know I'm not a strength and conditioning guy,'" Harden said. "But if you want to be the best you have to cross-train; you have to be an athlete, not a football player. Train like an Olympic athlete. That's what I tell anybody that will work with me.

"If you're a golfer and you're training like an Olympic athlete, who's going to beat you? Train like an athlete, not like a golfer. Train like an athlete, not like a football player. Train like an athlete, certainly not like a baseball player."

That summer, Howard's body underwent a total transformation. Not only did he add strength and muscle, he was now running cleaner pass routes, and his concentration was sharper. It all led to a remarkable statistic, something that never made it into the box scores, former UM receivers coach T.J. Weist said.

"Desmond only had four drops in game competition in 1991," said Weist, who charted every pass play in games, scrimmages and practices. Whenever Howard was on the line

A group of quarterbacks and receivers regularly worked out together in the summer of 1991, including (in front) Livetius Johnson and Elvis Grbac. (Standing) Ken Sollom, Desmond, Derrick Alexander, Julian Swearengin, John Ellison, Walter Smith, and Yale Van Dyne.

of scrimmage, opposite a defensive back, the result of that pass play was recorded.

"I believe he had 520 catches for the fall of 1991 – games, practices, everything – and only had 24 drops," said Weist, now the receivers coach at the University of Cincinnati.

"I always show my receivers those statistics. I say to them, 'You want to know why Desmond Howard won the Heisman? Look at this. He was amazing. You want to know why some receivers are great? They don't drop the ball.'

"Desmond just made play after play after play."

"Derrick Alexander was the primary punt return guy, and I ended up being the second returner. Well, we go into that first game at Boston College and Derrick Alexander blows his knee out. So they put me in, and the first college punt that I ever tried to catch — it seemed like that thing was up there for three days — I get nervous and fair catch that first one and everyone is like 20-yards away from me. They kick the second one, and again, it seems like it's around there for three days. I look out to see where everyone is at, and look back up and the ball hits the ground, and (the coaches) yank me like right away.

"Desmond goes in and the rest is history. So like I always say, if I wasn't such a freshman chump, and would have caught the punt and did well then, he wouldn't have had a chance to strike the Heisman pose."

TYRONE WHEATLEY
Michigan
Running Back, 1991-94; All-Big Ten, 1992-94

"There are some guys who are good. There are some guys who are great. And then there are some guys who are special. Desmond surpassed good and great while I watched him at Michigan. He was special, man, and I think you have to be special if you're going to be a Heisman Trophy winner."

JOE DUMARS
Detroit Pistons, President
Detroit Pistons Guard, 1985-99
Naismith Basketball Hall of Fame, 2006

DESMOND HOWARD Wide Receiver

Weldon said. "He's a great player and he had a fantastic year."

Howard was just the fourth winner who was not a running back or quarterback and the first Heisman winner from Michigan since Tom Harmon in 1940. Previously, only Southern California running back O.J. Simpson had won the Heisman by a wider margin, but there were fewer electors than who voted for Simpson over Purdue's Leroy Keyes in 1968. Howard won 85 percent of the first-place votes, three percent more than Simpson.

When his name was called, Howard was as much relieved, as he was excited. "It was a great feeling," he said. "We didn't know how the vote was going to go, because the year before, a lot of people assumed that Rocket Ismail of Notre Dame was going to win the award, and Ty Detmer actually won it. It was like, 'Hey, you never know how this thing is going to go, how these people out there feel about you, about your talent, about your school.' Then I thought, 'Maybe doing that pose might offend some people.' You never know."

It turned out that the voters valued Howard's poise far more than his pose. "Everybody stumbled except for Howard," noted Heisman voter Ivan Maisel of the Dallas Morning News. "All the other candidates took themselves out of the race."

Like frustrated defensive backs and irritated special teams cover men, Howard left them all in his wake.

5 WORKING WITH LEGENDS

Learning football and life lessons from Michigan's fabled coaches

"People need to realize that when they see coach Gary Moeller, they're looking at the man who went to Ohio and brought Michigan's last two Heisman Trophy winners back with him. That's big!"

DESMOND HOWARD
Hesiman Trophy Winner. 1991

The prospective recruit stared nervously at the name on the door. He felt small, insignificant, was overcome by nervousness and uncertainty. It wasn't so much the size of the door that was causing the uneasiness, as it was the enormity of the man on its other side.

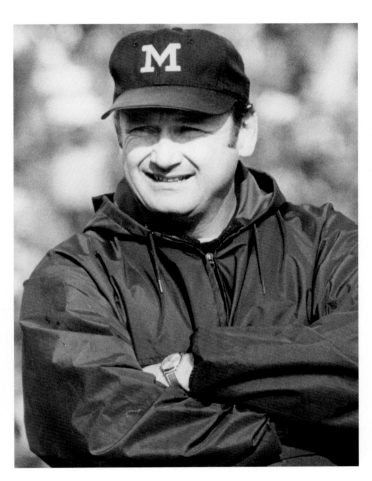

Desmond Howard, a Cleveland high school phenom and Michigan football hopeful, was about to knock on the door to the office of Wolverines legendary head coach Bo Schembechler, and there was a nauseous feeling in the pit of his stomach.

"It is intimidating," Howard said, remembering that day. "I was telling a friend of mine, what you have to understand is that Bo Schembechler is larger than life. There were few guys like him, where you'd say, 'That's Bo. That's (Penn State's Joe) Paterno. That's (Florida State's Bobby) Bowden. You just kind of step back and say, 'Wow.'

"There were few guys of that stature, who would command that type of response, just by walking in the room, or just by seeing them somewhere. I'm going to go in this door, and behind this door, is the great Bo Schembechler. You're looking at the door and you're trying to visualize everything. That was a crazy kind of surreal moment. I'm about to go through this door and meet *the* Bo Schembechler. Wow. There were a bunch of emotions going through me at a moment like that."

Howard's trepidation was understandable. Schembechler was, in fact, larger than life, not only on the Michigan campus, but across the college football world. Bo didn't just run Michigan football. Bo was Michigan football. Today, Schembechler still leads all Big Ten coaches with a winning percentage of .850 (143-24-3) in conference play.

Schembechler had an innate eye for character and ability, and almost immediately, he recognized that when it came to football, in Howard, he had discovered a unique specimen on both counts. "I think one of the quotes that I will cherish for the rest of my life came from Bo when he was asked about replacing the receivers they had before I got there," Howard said. "He was asked, 'John Kolesar, being a senior, how do you replace a guy

"I used to write my dad's name 'J.D.' on my tape before every game. So if things got tough, I would glance down at it for inspiration."

DESMOND HOWARD
Michigan
Wide Receiver, 1988-91
1991 Heisman Trophy Winner

"Desmond and I were really close and in the summer of 1990 we worked for the Detroit Police Department. We were working at these different apartment complexes and setting up like neighborhood watches where we would help older people with things like going to a store or whatever. Then we had these kids that were in the program run by the police department and we were like these camp counselors to them. I remember the things that we shared that summer were like of kids coming back having seen a dead body. These were some rough neighborhoods.

"One time there was this shootout in the neighborhood, and it really deepened our relationship. It was a Friday afternoon toward the end of the day, and these guys just started shooting. It was like a movie. You don't think how you will react in those situations, but I remember how calm we were because we had to get these kids away from there. Just seeing Desmond's eyes as we jumped under the desk, it was like, 'We've got to get out of here alive!'

"After, he got all of the kids together and told them to go home. He was selfless. And we only left after we knew the kids were safe. He was just so calm, but that's what you saw in him in all of the biggest games. ... So instead of saying how great of a football player Desmond was, what I remember most was just talking about life with Desmond. That's where he became my friend. It wasn't about the enormity of playing football at Michigan. It was always about life and what we were going to do after football. "

ON VAUGHN
Michigan
Tailback, 1988-90; All-Big Ten, 1990

like him?' And he said, 'Well, I've got this crafty little devil out of Cleveland named Desmond Howard and I think he's going to be something special.' He saw something in me that I didn't see at the time."

Howard's father, J.D., understood that Schembechler would be demanding of his son, and sent Desmond off to Michigan with a piece of advice – no matter how tough and difficult things might get that first year, don't complain. Don't come home from school whimpering about your lot in life. Suck it up and make the best of it.

That's exactly what Howard did, and the results speak for themselves, as does the lifelong bond he formed with Michigan's legendary head coach. "Bo Schembechler, he's my favorite coach of all-time," Howard said. "He's my favorite coach of any I've ever had. Going into the (College Football) Hall of Fame as one of his players, representing the University of Michigan is very significant to me."

Clearly, the feeling was mutual. Prior to the Gator Bowl at the conclusion of 1990 season, in which Michigan would face Mississippi, Schembechler, who'd retired and handed the coaching reins over to Gary Moeller at the start of that season, offered a word of wisdom to Mississippi free safety Todd Sandroni, who'd be charged with the task of covering Howard.

"You're in for a rough afternoon," Schembechler warned. He was right. Michigan won 35-3 and Howard scored on touchdown receptions of 63 and 50 yards.

When Schembechler died in 2006 at the age of 77, Howard was among the Michigan legends that returned for the memorial service at Michigan Stadium honoring Michigan's greatest legend. "Words cannot adequately describe the pain I felt at the loss of someone who I loved and admired so much," Howard said. "The Michigan family – along with the entire college football world – lost a giant. Bo was a man who shaped his young players into men both on and off the field."

The man who followed Schembechler faced an unenviable task, but Howard is steadfast in his respect and admiration for Moeller. "Gary is my guy," Howard said. "Coach Moeller, that's my guy. I can't say enough good things about him. He was so significant to the university and he loved the university. We really loved coach Moeller. He's a fantastic man, a great coach. A guy that I still love. I talk about him today and I tell people, 'Gary Moeller was a helluva coach.'"

It was Moeller who first recruited Howard for the Wolverines, winning out among some 20 schools to convince

DESMOND HOWARD
FUN FACTS

Howard was the 11th junior to win the Heisman Trophy, but the fourth in succession, following three future Detroit Lions - Barry Sanders of Oklahoma State (1988), Andre Ware of Houston (1989) and Ty Detmer of Brigham Young (1990).

him to come to Michigan. Once Howard was there, he was a youngster so overwhelmed by the vast array of talent on the field at practice during his freshman year that he originally set himself off into the pool of defensive backfield hopefuls. Moeller, who'd seen Howard in action in the high school ranks, gathered the freshman from among the safeties and convinced him to give wide receiver a try.

"We stood there and said, 'Yeah, he can catch the ball,'" Moeller recalled to Sports Illustrated in a 1991 interview. "It was just a quick pass, and then, first thing, he made a (tackler) miss. The one thing I liked about him early was he wanted the ball. He got mad when he didn't have the ball. He loved his hands on the ball."

Howard's love for what Moeller did at Michigan stems as much from how he sought to be his own man, and not simply try to do things the way Schembechler did. Moeller opened up Michigan's traditionally conservative offense to get the ball into the hands of players like Howard, and he also wasn't afraid to take risks. He lost to Michigan State when he opted to go for

a two-point conversion rather than settle for a tie, and he beat Notre Dame by having Elvis Grbac throw a TD pass to Howard on fourth and one.

"For what he did, I don't think people really understand it from our perspective as players," Howard said. "The way he coached that game against Notre Dame, or even the Michigan State game, the way he coached that game where the guy tripped me. Gary went for two. Gary wasn't going for the tie; he was going for the win. And then the next year, against Notre Dame, a fourth and one and he had enough confidence in Elvis and myself and our offense that throwing the ball wasn't just a mere possibility, it was a legitimate option.

"That goes a long way with players when they see they have a coach that has so much confidence and trust in their abilities that he's willing to put them in a position to win a game on fourth and one with a pass. No one saw that coming. No one ever imagined we'd go to the end zone. We went for it all. To show that type of confidence in us that early in the season meant everything. You rarely ever see a young coach take a risk like that in the second

"At that time, we had a lot of teams that were ranked nationally in the top 15 — football, basketball, hockey, gymnastics, baseball, wrestling — so there were a lot of quote-unquote stars that were walking around campus, but of course nobody bigger than Desmond.

"We used to go to the CCRB to play basketball and outside of South Quad; Desmond could play. I just remember him being fast as hell. I remember him getting out onto the wing, running fast and beating everybody up and down the court getting lay-ups. He had a quick first-step, a very explosive first-step. But when Desmond and I used to play together I don't think we ever lost. Matter of fact, we played in a (2010) charity game and he still has wheels. He's just a natural athlete and I think Desmond is the type of guy who will be a 70-year-old guy racing 20-year-olds some day and still giving them a run."

JIMMY KING
Michigan Basketball
Guard. 1991-95

THE BACK STORY

Howard's best acrobatic catch — ever!

Desmond Howard was excited beyond words.

His college roommate, Marc Jacobson, had scored a pair of tickets – third row center – to one of three sold-out Michael Jackson shows in late October 1988 at the Palace of Auburn Hills.

Unfortunately, for Marc, he came down ill the day of the concert. Not wanting to disappoint his friend, he gave the tickets to Desmond and told him to enjoy himself. And finding a taker for the other ticket wasn't difficult, in fact, the first guy he asked, Tripp Welborne, jumped at the opportunity to see Jackson's Bad Tour pull into suburban Detroit.

"Both of us were big Michael Jackson fans, I mean, after all, he was the greatest of all time, so you have to respect that, just like Muhammad Ali," Welborne said.

When the song "Billie Jean" started, Welborne, who had watched the video of the live performance enough times on MTV, remembered the King of Pop tossing the black Fedora into the crowd on the song's final note.

"Sure enough, as Michael sings the last line of the song, he throws his hat out into the crowd," Welborne said. "That hat is spinning in the air like a Frisbee. … And it's coming our way! For the both of us everything was really, really going in slow motion. Des and I, at the same time, dive for the hat, which was crazy since all we were used to diving for was footballs."

It was pitch-black in the arena, and there were two UM teammates – Welborne even sporting a cast to protect a fractured wrist – diving into an aisle for a chance to capture a piece of pop culture history.

Simultaneously, the pair grabbed hold of the hat and landed hard on the concrete floor. Meanwhile, other concertgoers jumped into the fray with hopes of wrangling the hat away from the Michigan duo.

"We lay out like in a baseball game trying to catch a ball, and we land on several people in front of us," Welborne recalled. "The house lights come up and they put this spotlight on the pile, and people start to realize that we have the hat. But we're on the bottom of the pile and Des and I each have two hands on it."

game of the season on national television. We had a new found respect for coach Moeller after that game."

There was another institution on campus that Howard revered and respected – the place where he got to play. "Michigan Stadium – I don't think it gets any better," Howard said. "I can't see any better scenario than that. I really can't."

Howard still vividly recalls the first time he ran out on that field for a game in front of 100,000 fans. "I was a young kid, a redshirt freshman just taking it all in, enjoying the moment," he said. "It's definitely special, because it's such an obviously significant stadium, the biggest stadium in the country. You're representing the maize and blue. There's a big difference when you go out there as a redshirt freshman, not expecting to play, as opposed to knowing that you're going to be in the thick of the action; It's a whole different mentality. You're not going out there to spectate; you're going out to participate. I remember running down the tunnel, jumping up to hit that banner, there's a giddiness behind it. But the mind-blowing part was the first time I ran down the tunnel and saw how it opened up to a sea of maize and blue. … What a beautiful site.

"It's crazy."

Arena security finally arrived to help remove people from the pile, when, Welborne said, "There was Desmond with his million-watt smile, and holding the hat up as if we had just won the national championship."

Three years later, shortly after Howard made his famously acrobat diving touchdown catch against Notre Dame, he told a Sports Illustrated reporter that the hat-grab was the greatest catch of his collegiate career.

"To this day, there are a couple of displays at Desmond's house,"

said Welborne, a two-time All-America strong safety at Michigan. "Obviously, there's the Super Bowl MVP, and then there's the Heisman Trophy, but I think the most prominent display is the Michael Jackson hat."

Howard had four dropped passes during the 1991 season, but he sure wasn't going to let go of his most cherished Michael Jackson memento.

"It's funny because we were supposed to share the hat 50/50 between our houses," Welborne said. "Originally it went to his house in Cleveland, because it was a lot closer than my house in North Carolina. We drove it down there. That was the first stop, 2 ½ hours away.

"But now I joke with him that (the hat) made it to the first stop and it never left the first stop. It's just been traveling with him. It's never stopped off at my trophy case. Now I just live vicariously with the Michael Jackson hat through Desmond."

"It's an unbelievable story. I think for both of us coming from Ohio going to Michigan, both of us winning the Heisman Trophy, both of us playing together in Oakland, then both of us winning the Super Bowl with the Green Bay Packers at two different times. I told him just recently, 'All I have to do is follow Desmond's career and I'll be successful.' I think I'm doing well. I'm just going to continue following him, and when I retire I'm going to give him a call so we can figure out what steps I should take next.

"Getting the chance to play with him in Oakland was a great experience. You grow up watching the guy, but you never expect that you'll play with him. This was a guy that I watched for many years as a Wolverine and I cheered for. And now here we are together in Oakland. It was a treat because Desmond is a guy who always has a positive attitude and has become a very good friend, so it was just a pleasure for me to be around him."

CHARLES WOODSON
Michigan
Cornerback, 1995-97, Heisman Trophy Winner, 1997

DESMOND HOWARD
FUN FACTS

During the 1998 National Football League season with the Oakland Raiders, among
Howard's teammates was rookie defensive back Charles Woodson, the 1997 Heisman
Trophy winner at Michigan and the first defensive player to win the Heisman

6 MANY HAPPY RETURNS

Howard's electric kick returns turn him into a football legend

Whether it's Wayne Gretzky finding a seam in a seemingly clogged attacking zone, or Magic Johnson dishing off a no-look pass for an easy basket, there's something all the greats of sports share — a special vision, an ability to see the playing field that the ordinary player simply does not possess.

I t was no different with Desmond Howard. When he returned a kick, he was Picasso carrying a pigskin. An artist like no other. Returning to him wasn't merely a job; it was a work of art.

"For me, I'd focus on a portion of the field, with the rest of field in my peripheral vision," Howard said, trying to explain what it's like to be the world's best return man. "Once I catch it, I take a quick mental snapshot of the whole field, so then I know how things are laid out. If it's a left return, I'll focus in on that portion of the field. If it's a middle return, my main focus is right in front of me, but I'm always aware of what's going on around me. If the ball is kicked to the left, during a middle return, that works to my advantage because I can easily focus on the part of the field the return is designed to go. Vision is a key component in becoming a great return man.

"The purpose of the snapshot of the whole field is so I'll know where the would-be tacklers are going to be coming from. With that information I can gauge how much time I have to get away from the people who are next to me. And I also get a better sense of where the next wave of would-be tacklers will come from. Making the first guy miss is a must. After that, I'm looking to pick up blocks from my guys in an attempt to find a lane.

"Once I get in the open field, there's a sense of accomplishment – a rush, because I know what's ahead. I'm going to score a touchdown and I want to get there as fast as possible. I want to make sure that moment happens.

"I just loved to hear the crowd ooh and aah when I got the ball. I loved to hear the hush as the ball came to me, and then the roar when I took off."

Howard made his mark as a return man at Michigan, a combination of electricity, raw ability, elusiveness and blazing speed that could turn the ordinary into a once-in-a-lifetime play.

"When I first began playing football I was timid, apprehensive, afraid to 'layout' for the ball in the same way I had watched Desmond do so many times. However, as I continued to watch him dive for catch after catch, leading up to his famous Heisman pose, I began to see the field of green grass as a giant green pillow, and footballs as though they were some of the most valuable and precious pieces of jewels on the face of the earth, which were never to be dropped. Watching Desmond Howard's diving catches in the maize and blue is what ultimately made the game of football look fun and exciting to me."

IAN GOLD
Michigan
Running Back, 1996-97; Linebacker, 1998-99

"He excelled at returning kicks, and that was no easy job," remembered former Michigan head coach Lloyd Carr, an assistant coach on the staffs of Bo Schembechler and Gary Moeller when Howard was with the Wolverines. "You've got to watch the ball and catch it with 11 men coming down the field intent on tackling you. And yet he managed to elude the coverage so many times. He was probably the most exciting player I ever saw.

"If Desmond had the ball in his hands, you didn't take your eyes off of him, because something spectacular could happen at any moment."

During his Michigan career, Howard returned two kickoffs for touchdowns – a 95-yard return to the house against Michigan State in 1990 and a 93-yard runback against Boston College in 1991. The two kick return touchdowns remain a school career record. His final touchdown as a Wolverine was a school-record 93-yard punt return score against Ohio State, which he punctuated with his famous Heisman Trophy pose in the Buckeyes' end zone. In 2006, EA Sports honored

Howard by putting him on the cover of its NCAA Football 06 video game, utilizing his Heisman pose as its cover art.

When he reached the NFL, it was Howard's ability as a return man that allowed him to stand out in the crowd in the world's best football league. As a pro, he returned eight punts for touchdowns, which places Howard in a tie for fourth all-time in NFL history in that department with Rick Upchurch and Jack Christiansen. His NFL career per-return average of 11.9 yards is good for 11th overall all-time.

His first score as a pro was a 58-yard punt return touchdown for the Washington Redskins against the Atlanta Falcons in 1992, his rookie season. Toward the end of his 11-year NFL career, Moeller, Howard's old coach at Michigan, helped bring

"Back to Back"

"Obviously, you'd seen him on TV with all of those great highlights. He wasn't the biggest guy, but I think watching him play and stepping up in big games — whether it was a punt return or a reception — I just had a lot of respect for the way he played.

"Then when he struck the pose, I thought at the time and the circumstances when he did it, it was probably well deserved. It put an exclamation point on his season. It was kind of late enough in the season that everyone knew that he was the guy that would win it. I didn't think it was showboating. I just think it showed how much he enjoyed playing and enjoyed the game. He had a flair for the dramatic, so it was like icing on the cake for him. He trademarked that one."

TY DETMER
Brigham Young
Quarterback, 1987-91; Heisman Trophy Winner, 1990

DESMOND HOWARD
FUN FACTS

The Washington Redskins traded with the Cincinnati Bengals to acquire the No. 4 overall pick in the 1992 NFL draft, which they then used to select Howard.

"I remember the first time I tackled him. It was the second game of the (1992) season when we played the Redskins. I remember coming out onto RFK Stadium for pre-game and seeing him running routes. I thought to myself, 'Man, this guy is small.' It was the second quarter, and they ran a wide receiver reverse where he went in motion out to the left side of the field. He came back in motion across when they snapped the ball. The quarterback gave him the ball and I shot the gap and grabbed him from behind right in the middle of his shoulder pads in the back. ... The timing was perfect.

"And then there was an incident where he ran one back for us. I can't remember if he ran one back for six-points, or he got it into the red zone. But when he came off the field everyone on the sideline was so excited, I mean the Silverdome was erupting. I went over to congratulate him, and in my excitement I hit him in the head, smacking him like, 'Good job!' But I hit him too hard, and it hurt his neck and he fell out on the field. I didn't knock him out, but he was on a knee. He was out, but not unconscious out. He had to get attention from the trainers, and I think he missed the next game because of that.

"But he was always electrifying, man! He was always doing something exciting. Man, he had the million dollar smile and whenever they showed him on the sideline or in the end zone, he just looked like he was having a lot of fun."

ROBERT PORCHER
Detroit Lions
Defensive Tackle, 1992-2003

CLEVELAND BROWNS · **Detroit Lions** ·

GAMEDAY

$5.00

Gerard Warren Ignites the Defense
page 10

Desmond Howard Comes Home to Cleveland
page 4

GIANT EAGLE

"We had nobody. I told Bobby Ross that Desmond Howard was on the street after being released by Green Bay a few days earlier. I told Bobby, 'We can get Desmond.' I had Corwin Brown call him. He got a hold of him in Chicago. We flew him to Detroit. We had to get him to Detroit and sign him before four o'clock for him to be eligible to play for us on Sunday against Washington. That night we introduced him to the team. If I remember correctly, his signing with us may not have made the Sunday morning paper. But when they introduced him before that first punt of the game in the Silverdome, a lot of people were surprised. The place went crazy. And then he returned that first punt for a 68-yard touchdown. It's a truly remarkable story."

CHUCK PRIEFER
Detroit Lions
Special Teams Coach, 1997-2006

"I like him as a broadcaster. I remember talking to him when he first took on the position. First I thought it was funny. I was like, 'Com'on! What is Desmond going to get on TV and talk about?' If you know him, he's just this character; he laughs all of the time. He jokes all of the time, and you see these other guys on TV and you can tell that they're intense about it when they are commentating. I just couldn't see Desmond doing that. But now you see him, he's perfect. It leads right into his character and the type of person that he is. I think he brings energy and that glow to the show. I really enjoy watching him. I think he's doing a fantastic job."

HERMAN MOORE
Detroit Lions
Wide Receiver, 1991-2002

When it came to football, it was always mind over matter for Howard

Before he played organized football, Desmond Howard had already acquired a knack for making older, big guys look ridiculous on the playground at Gracemount Elementary School in Cleveland.

"It was just amazing," recalled Jonathan Jones Sr., Desmond's older brother. "I remember my friends and I would try to hit the little guy out of anger, and instead we were left to stand there and just watch him."

Having a younger brother shadow him through the neighborhood wasn't always a delight for Jonathan. In fact, sometimes it was a real drag, Jonathan said. But those were his parents' rules. So if Jonathan wanted to play with his friends, well, then he had to let Desmond tag along.

"Of course, Desmond played against older guys, my friends," Jonathan said. "That put Desmond at an advantage later in terms of a maturity factor. He was now getting a grasp of things more than kids his own age, which was good because we weren't doing the bad things. I was an older brother who was focused on athletics and academics, so they were going to follow in my foot-steps."

In the summers, Jonathan and his friends would play football on a grassy plot of land next to the elementary school, which was about one mile from the Howard's home on Stockbridge Avenue. The challenge then for any ball-carrier was not to be tackled into the metal railings, which divided the grass from the concrete sidewalk.

"The railings were our out-of-bounds," Jonathan said. "I would never try to hurt him, but there was this big brother-little brother thing where I would try to hurt him a little bit. So you always tried to hit him where the railing was, just so he would wake up and see reality."

However, the truth of the matter was Desmond was lightning fast. And once he figured out how to make guys miss, he had become practically untouchable.

"With that came the agility because he could run right around us and not worry about that rail," Jonathan said. "If he had to, he could jump that rail, miss being tackled, come back in and complete the touchdown."

Once Desmond gained the confidence, nothing was going to slow him down. Not even a common psychological practice used by one of his college coaches.

Former Michigan wide receivers coach T.J. Weist said that he preferred to test his receivers' mettle prior to the start of the season. He would purposely try to get his players to quit the team in order to test their mental toughness.

But Desmond wasn't so easy.

"You try to make workouts as hard as they can be to make them quit," said Weist, who coached at Michigan from 1990-93. "You yell at players and put them in hard situations to make them break. You do this because you don't want them to break in a game with the pressure.

"And the one thing I could never do was break Desmond. Couldn't break him. Didn't matter how much you turned the heat up or put pressure on him, especially mentally. Other guys, you could make them quit. But Desmond was unique; you couldn't break him and that smile."

Even when he reached the NFL, the land of behemoth men hell-bent on destruction and violence, Desmond rose above. He played 11 seasons, scored 15 touchdowns and amassed 12,519 all-purpose yards, which ranks third all-time among players from the 1992 draft class.

Even Tim Brown, the 1987 Heisman Trophy winner from Notre Dame and nine-time Pro Bowl return specialist for the Los Angeles/Oakland Raiders, marveled at Howard's abilities.

"This is a guy who has the body, the mind and the ability to make it happen," said Brown, of Howard. "And he always did things more courageously than I did. My first move was always laterally. But he was always the opposite. His first step was always right up the center of the field, and I used to admire that."

him back to the state when he was an assistant coach of the Detroit Lions, and two of Howard's last three NFL scores were punt-return touchdowns for Detroit.

But it was the 1996 season, when Howard was playing for the Green Bay Packers, which would prove to be his most glorious campaign as a pro. During the season, Howard shattered the NFL record for return yards in a season with 875. His 15.1 yards per punt return was the best in the league. He became the first player in 15 years to return three punts for touchdowns in a season, and the only player in Packers' history to do it. "A lot of times, he gets us to the 50-yard line," receiver Antonio Freeman, Green Bay's return man in 1995, told The Associated Press. "If you cut the field down that much, it's easy coming in."

In the playoffs, Howard ramped up his return game to unprecedented levels. During a 35-14 rout of the San Francisco 49ers, Howard's two punt returns – one for 46 yards and another for 71 yards and a touchdown – in a cold rain in Green Bay's division playoff victory were back breakers for the Niners.

He didn't score during Green Bay's 35-13 NFC Championship win over the Carolina Panthers, but Howard would take control of the game in Super Bowl XXXI against the New England Patriots.

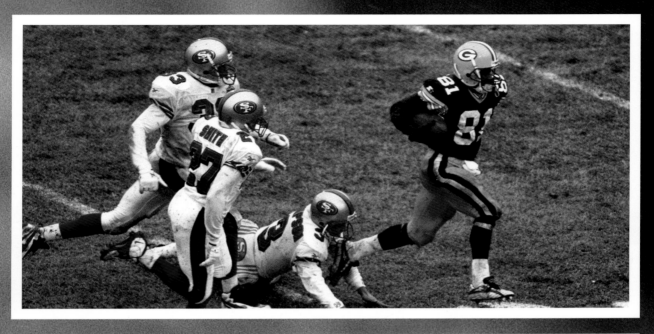

DESMOND HOWARD
FUN FACTS

Howard was the second wide receiver to win the Heisman. Tim Brown of Notre Dame (1987), later Howard's teammate with the Oakland Raiders, was the first

Even his opponents in the big game couldn't take their eyes off of Howard. "Every time we punt the ball, I'm definitely going to be watching him," Patriots return specialist David Meggett told the New York Times on the eve of the Super Bowl. "He thrills me."

Earlier in the game, he'd come close to breaking a big one, returning punts for 32 and 33 yards. But late in the third quarter, with Green Bay clinging to a 27-21 lead, Howard would put the dagger through the hearts of the Patriots.

Receiving the kickoff after a New England touchdown, Howard raced straight up the middle of the field and into the clear. He stopped at the one-yard line, then emphatically stomped a foot into the end zone to put an exclamation point on what would be a 35-21 Packers victory.

When it was over, Howard made more history. He was named Super Bowl MVP, the first special teams player to be honored,

and just the fourth player in football history to have won the Heisman Trophy and be named Super Bowl MVP.

"I really didn't expect them to kick me the ball that much," Howard said, recalling his memorable Super Bowl performance. "But as I've said before, you could roll the dice and kick it to me if you want. But if you kept doing it, you were going to get burned eventually."

E GATE · 328 SECTION · 17 ROW · 17 SEAT
LOGE

Super Bowl XXXI
New Orleans

AFC-NFC WORLD CHAMPIONSHIP GAME
SUNDAY, JANUARY 26, 1997 · 5:00 P.M.
LOUISIANA SUPERDOME
NEW ORLEANS

$275 ALL TAXES INCLUDED
GATES OPEN AT 2:00 P.M.

"To not be the quarterback and actually influence the games as much as he did — and obviously that's the reason he won the Heisman Trophy — is when you can be on the field in a bunch of different ways and you effect the game like he did, not touching the ball every play like a quarterback does, it was amazing. When you watched Michigan, anytime that there was a punt return you had to sit and watch because you knew that something special was going to happen. And a lot of times it did."

GINO TORRETTA
Miami (Fla.)
Quarterback, 1989-92; Heisman Trophy Winner, 1992

7 A MICHIGAN MAN FOREVER

Howard carries the Wolverines spirit into life after football

THE HEISMAN MEMORIAL TROPHY

DESMOND K. HOWARD
UNIVERSITY OF MICHIGAN

When Desmond Howard called a news conference at Crisler Arena for Jan. 21, 1992, every Michigan fan knew what it was about. Howard was leaving school to pursue the National Football League, but suggestions that he left school early still make Howard bristle.

F or me, there wasn't anything else left to do," he said. "In the classroom, I graduated. People were saying that 'Desmond left college early,' and I would always kind of feel it was hypocritical, because if they were honest in how they viewed student-athletes, the student is first. I took care of that part. I graduated, and anyone else who graduated from college, you just expect them to go out and seek employment once they graduate. That's what I did. I graduated and went out and sought employment, and that was with the NFL.

"Just because I had a year of eligibility left on the football field, that doesn't mean I left school early. The definition of a kid who leaves school early is that he didn't get his degree. I graduated. I got my degree. On the field, there was nothing new that I could have done – maybe break a few more records, but as far as awards and accolades are concerned, once you've won the Heisman, then most people in college football think you've done it all."

Howard was selected fourth overall by the Washington Redskins in the 1992 NFL draft and went on to play an 11-season career in the league with Washington, the Jacksonville Jaguars, Green Bay Packers, Oakland Raiders and Detroit Lions.

Since concluding his playing career after the 2002 season, he has been inducted into the Greater Cleveland Sports Hall of Fame, the Gator Bowl Hall of Fame, the University of Michigan Hall of Honor, and the State of Michigan Sports Hall of Fame. The Desmond Howard/Pat Richter award has gone to the Big Ten's top receiver since 2010.

That same year, Howard was presented with college football's greatest post-career achievement when he was announced as one of the inductees into the College Football Hall of Fame.

"It was an unbelievable honor," Howard said. "It's one of those things that just seemed so surreal. It covers your whole body of work in college and shows that there's a certain level

Desmond and fellow Michigan alum, Glen Rice, entered the Michigan Sports Hall of Fame as members of the induction class of 2009.

Former wide receiver Matt Eiseman, who played on the same Vikings teams with Desmond, shared a laugh together in the St. Joseph gymnasium during an event held to retire Howard's No. 27 shortly after he won the Heisman.

DESMOND HOWARD
FUN FACTS

Howard scored the first touchdown in Jacksonville Jaguars history, a 15-yard scoring reception from quarterback Mark Brunell against the Houston Oilers on Oct. 1, 1995. It was the winning score with 1:03 to play in a 17-16 victory, also the first in franchise history.

of respect for what you were able to accomplish in college. For me, it's always a tremendous honor to be inducted into anything of national significance. And representing the University of Michigan in doing it, going into the College Football Hall of Fame as a Michigan Wolverine, it doesn't get any better for me."

Howard fondly recalls the moment he got the news, because of who broke the news to him – his mother. "The way I got the news was my mom had called," he said. "I was working out and I couldn't really hear that clearly because the music was going on in the background. I ended up turning it down and I said, 'What are you saying now?'

"My mom, she can mess up a story. She can have the facts, but she can get them all twisted up. She said, 'Baby, you did it again.' And I said, 'What momma? What are you talking about? What did I do? What happened?' She said, 'You did it. A man called and you're going to be in the hall of fame.' I was thinking maybe he said that I was going to be on the ballot, which I already knew.

"It was kind of early, because I was just put on the ballot the year before. Sometimes, those things take time. I said, 'Give me

"The focus for Ohio State, obviously, had to be with stopping Desmond, and slowing him down. I can see the punt right now. It was actually a really good punt. The first guy down missed him, and the rest of that play was Des being Des. He did something that probably only a few people alive could do, and I don't think anybody got a finger on him.

"I was standing at about the 25-yard line and he was running right towards me. I was two feet from the sidelines, and I looked into his eyes and thought, 'Wow, this is really about to happen.' Things were moving so slow because of my vantage point, that he just pulled away from everybody. Then he pulled the pose out. I think that happened too fast that it really didn't hit you like, 'Did he just do that?' Then of course you go back and see all of the replays of what became the signature play of his career."

KIRK HERBSTREIT
Ohio State
Quarterback, 1989-92; Co-Captain, 1992
ESPN 'College GameDay' Analyst

"Desmond was one of the few players, who would want to sometimes watch the game from our suite, because he was so immersed in learning. It's no secret to us why he's such a great person on television now, because he would come to the games and want to hear what we were seeing, what we were watching. He was always asking questions. He wanted to ask Joe Dumars and I questions about the NBA and basketball in general, and why things are. He wasn't just coming to watch the game and go home; it was almost as if every game he came to he was trying to learn something from it."

GEORGE DAVID
Detroit Pistons, Director of Player Personnel

the guy's name and number and I'll give him a call,' to make sure what she was telling me was accurate. Just to hear the happiness and how proud she was in her voice as she spoke, it made me feel good. I was more or less hoping that she was right. I made the phone call and it was true."

Today a college football analyst for ESPN, Howard admits that he doesn't spend a lot of time dwelling on his accomplishments at Michigan. "I don't think about it unless someone brings it up," he said. "I'm so busy now covering college football for a living, doing speaking engagements, I don't really think about those years. I hope I'm not at that age yet where I start spending my time thinking of those old accomplishments."

The day the Hall of Fame called, though, all of those thrills and achievements came flooding to the forefront of his memory bank. "After that, you start to think about it," Howard said. "It's easier to think about something when a lot of people around you start talking about it, and that's what happened. I have pictures hanging up that remind me of some of those special moments. I think about the players, I think about the coaches."

"As I look back, he was a happy-go-lucky, smiling kid in school. As the 1991 season went on, I'm not sure that any of us totally appreciated just what he was doing and how far he could go, including his teammates. I always got the feeling, whether I was talking to him, or I heard other interviews, that he never viewed himself as a Heisman Trophy contender because wide receivers don't win the Heisman Trophy.

"I guarantee you that I didn't appreciate it until he struck that pose after the punt return against Ohio State. That's when it really struck me that he might win this thing now. You just saw this progression of him from just another guy on the team to becoming this true superstar of college football. It happened through performance, not through a marketing campaign, or anything like that.

"From my standpoint, I'm really proud of the way he's grown into the broadcast profession. I think he's become very, very good at what he does as a college football commentator. I think he can be an outstanding color commentator. He's a sharp guy, he's a witty guy and think the sky's the limit in this profession for him too."

FRANK BECKMANN
Michigan Football Broadcaster

"I dated Desmond's best friend's cousin, and she lived in his neighborhood. I needed a haircut and his friend was a barber. So a friend of mine and I are in the basement getting our hair cut by Marcus (Greene), that was Desmond's friend. While I'm sitting there, someone said, 'This is my man right here, Desmond Howard. He's going to win the Heisman Trophy.' You know, back then I was a young street kid — 23 or 24 — and I didn't think anybody from the hood, but me, was going to make it. I was so arrogant back then.

"I looked at him and said, 'Get out of here! You're no ballplayer!' My friend and I were ready to jump on Desmond. We didn't believe them, and we're cursing him up and down.

"I didn't see Desmond for quite awhile after that. Then I went to prison in 1992, and this guy came to visit me in prison and when I came home from prison, he was the first guy at my house. Before then he made that unbelievable Heisman Trophy pose and the country went crazy, and here I am, the heavyweight champion of the world, and I'm telling people that I know that kid, 'He's a friend of my girl's cousin.' And they're

like, 'He just came on the scene. You don't know him, Mike, you've been locked up!' Here I am — an international figure — and these guys didn't believe that I knew Desmond.

"But the thing that I want to say more than anything is that Desmond is one of the most awesome individuals that I have ever met. He's one of the guys that I will never forget. He's such a gentleman. He's just a wonderful guy. You could be having a miserable day, but when you see him things change. He's just a very special individual. I've been through everything in my life

but this guy is never judgmental about anything. He's a beautiful human being, and he makes us know what it's like to be a good human being.

"When we were telling him that he wasn't no football player, he was just laughing. We even got mad and told him to stop lying to us. But he wasn't threatened at all, and here I am, the heavyweight champion, telling him to stop lying. ... But this guy is so awesome."

MIKE TYSON
Former Boxer, 1985-2005
Undisputed World Heavyweight Champion, 1987-90

A pair of College Football Hall of Famers: Desmond with USC's Lynn Swann, who was inducted in 1993.

A pair of Cleveland St. Joseph alums: Desmond with one half of the Golic brothers, Bob, who graduated in 1975.

DESMOND HOWARD
FUN FACTS

After scoring on a 92-yard punt return for the Green Bay Packers in a 31-3 rout of
the Detroit Lions at the Pontiac Silverdome, Howard struck his Heisman Trophy
pose in the end zone. "It was just impulsive," he said.

Jonathan Jones Jr. with his Uncle Magic and comic book character Wolverine.

Howard also thinks often about his family. He and his wife, Rebkah, reside in Miami, Florida. They have a daughter, Sydney, and twin boys, Dhamir and Desmond Jr.

He's one of four sons to his parents, J.D. and Hattie, and all are successes in their own right. Oldest brother Jonathan served as an Air Force mechanic in the first Gulf War. Youngest brother Jermaine, who followed Desmond to St. Joseph High School, works as a computer engineer. And Chad, the second of the four brothers, is simply known by the family as Mr. Fix It.

"Plumber is his official title, but he's much more than a plumber," Howard said. "People have different gifts, and Chad's gifts are his hands, and what he can do with them. There's not much he can't fix.

Desmond lives in Miami with his family (from left), Desmond Jr., Sydney, Rebkah and Dhamir.

"I'm not the most mechanically gifted person. I'm not the one to be fixing machines and things like that. Chad walked me through fixing my washing machine, my toilet and my dishwasher, all three of those things, on the telephone. That's a talent. I didn't know what I was doing, but he was so detailed with it that I couldn't mess it up. I can follow instructions really well. I can take coaching. Outside of that, I would have been totally useless with the right tools and a broken dishwasher."

Then there's that maize and blue family in Ann Arbor that Howard will always hold close to his heart.

"I'm a Michigan Man forever," he said. "A great sense of pride may be an understatement. I don't even know if they have a word to actually capture that feeling.

"The Big House is extraordinary because of the men who coached in that stadium – Coach Schembechler, Coach Moeller, Coach Carr, and those before them, who set the stage and established the tradition. Then you add remarkable players like Tom Harmon, Anthony Carter, Charles Woodson and countless others.

"I'm just proud to have been able to contribute to the memorable times we've been able to give our fans in that stadium. Without these coaches and players – it's just a structure. We're put there to create those breathtaking moments, those special fall afternoons that fans of the game live for and likely remember for the rest of their lives. That's what makes the Big House special. I consider myself extremely fortunate to have played at the University of Michigan, and am humbled whenever I am reminded that I've provided highlights and memories that have stood the test of time, and will likely live for generations to come. It is, by far, one of the most significant accomplishments of my life."

"He's engaging and has a great personality with the smile and the laugh. But you know, I think there's obvious substance behind the smile. I think that he's tough and when you see him you think, 'God, how did you do what you did?' I think that's amazing. He won't tell you what you want to hear; he will tell you what he feels and you can take it or you can argue it; do whatever you want with it."

GINO TORRETTA
Miami (Fla.)
Quarterback, 1989-92;
Heisman Trophy Winner, 1992

THE BACK STORY

Howard's legacy continues to burn bright

His name is firmly inscribed on nearly every conceivable award that a college football player can win, including the Heisman Trophy. Yet Desmond Howard's greatest contributions to Michigan and the football world reaches far beyond the gridiron.

For legions of college football fans, his many acrobatic touchdown catches and dazzling kick returns will forever be preserved in the annals of college athletics. And decades from now the name 'Desmond Howard' will still be trivialized on television game shows. However, Desmond's legacy is much more than aging video highlights on YouTube and answers on "Jeopardy".

Those who know him best will always cherish Desmond as much, much more. To them, he's a loving father, devoted husband, treasured son, brother, nephew, uncle, and loyal friend.

Even when business obligations occasionally present challenges, Desmond doesn't make excuses for those closest to him. He makes time. And now that his oldest brother's son has chosen to travel a similar path into professional sports, Desmond is there to mentor and guide him on his journey.

"He's great for me to ask advice," said Jonathan Jones Jr., Desmond's nephew, who is an outfielder in the Toronto Blue Jays minor-league system. "He's always willing to talk; he's always willing to help, and that means a lot to me."

One particular conversation, Jones recalls, is when he asked his uncle about redshirting. It was early 2008, toward the start of Jones's freshman baseball season at Long Beach State. Like his uncle, Jonathon struggled in his first collegiate year.

"I wasn't playing much," Jonathan said. "I was like the only kid on the team without an at-bat. I asked my uncle what he thought about redshirting. He said, 'Hey, it worked out for me.' I didn't know that he redshirted for his freshman year. I just took his advice and after that I ended up not redshirting, and I had one of my best seasons ever."

Jonathan finished his first season as the Dirtbags' second-leading hitter with a .343 batting average.

"He's just such a good person to go to because he's been through it all," said Jonathan, of his uncle. "I will always remember how he was when me and my younger brother, Juliene, were around. There aren't a lot of athletes who take the time that he does and give back. When you find an athlete like him – and he's my uncle, coming from the same blood – it's special."

Transitioning from his post-playing career, Desmond remains an outstanding ambassador for Michigan and its football program. Whether it's on the set of ESPN's "College GameDay" or giving a speech to a gathering of business executives, Desmond is still synonymous with the true spirit of Michigan and what it means to be a Michigan Man.

"He's so special. He's something rare," said former Michigan basketball star Juwan Howard.

When Juwan Howard entered the NBA and struggled to make it in a strange city as a rookie, Desmond – who experienced similar tribulations two-years earlier with the Redskins – offered help to a fellow Michigan alumnus.

"Once I joined the Washington Bullets, Desmond reached out to me to lend his support and open up his house to me," Juwan Howard said. "I really appreciated that, and he certainly didn't have to do that. But it goes to show you that he's not only great at his craft, he's a great person."

It's that engaging personality, which makes Desmond approachable and an influential source for his television colleagues, like fellow Heisman Trophy winner Andre Ware.

"When I have a question, or need a comment on something that's happened, he's the first guy I call on the phone," said Ware, a college football analyst. "I probably have a closer relationship with Desmond than I do with anybody at ESPN."

Like Desmond's nephew says, "He's been a tremendous help to me just as far as the struggles of life, of professional sports. … He's Uncle Magic to me."

And the legacy lives on!

8

A
TRIBUTE
TO THE
LEGEND

The College Football Hall

On a beautiful sun-drenched afternoon in mid-July, the final chapter of Desmond Howard's illustrious football career was written when he took his rightful place along side 895 other players who are forever enshrined in the College Football Hall of Fame. In doing so, Howard became the 35th Michigan Man to earn induction to the hall in South Bend, IN.

Shortly after the inductees received their official blazers during an outside ceremony in Gridiron Plaza, one of the presentation co-hosts tried to get Howard to strike "The Pose."

With a bashful smile, Howard politely declined, saying, "It's something that I'm asked to do all of the time now. But that was a special moment at a special place for a special crowd. So I've decided to leave that in Ann Arbor for that crowd that witnessed it. I don't want to cheapen it by doing it everywhere else I go."

Later, at the enshrinement dinner, Howard thanked his "coaches" for charting the course to becoming more than a Hall of Fame football player, but a bright student, and loving father and husband.

"My first coaches were my parents, my mom, Hattie, and my dad, J.D.," Desmond said. "My teammates were my brothers. And together they set the foundation. … It took off for me under the system of Bo Schembechler. I've called him one-of-one: none before him, none to come. He's one of a kind. I was blessed to have played for him, and then for Gary Moeller, who was an extension of Bo. They carried on that similar thread of hard-work, discipline, and sacrifice. … It was that common theme of teamwork and it all started with my parents."

"Desmond was probably the only bright spot in that whole deal, because we sucked. They brought in players with great winning attitudes and winning traditions, but the team didn't have players that believed in each other. It was hard, and I don't have any good memories of my experiences in Detroit, other than Desmond and his incredible work ethic. We were hoping that other people would try to emulate that. ... Man, he just has the smile, which is the first thing that you notice about Desmond. His smile warms you up, and he's just a great personality. And then his athleticism, here's a man who can get it done. He's a joy to be around."

CHARLES HALEY
James Madison University, Linebacker, 1982-85
Detroit Lions Defensive Line Coach, 2001-02
Class of 2011
College Football Hall of Fame

DESMOND HOWARD
UNIVERSITY OF MICHIGAN 1989-1991

"When you're a Heisman Trophy winner, you're the face of college football forever. You're immortalized, let's be honest. He's charismatic, we all know that he's talented, he's a great guy, and he's the perfect face for college football because he's got that smile and that contagious energy. He's a class act and just a thrill to be around. ... I just wish that I could have done more with him as a wide receiver in the one year that I had him with the Raiders. I was a young coach back then, so that's my fault."

JON GRUDEN
Desmond's coach with Oakland Raiders in 1998

During the blazer presentation at the College Football Hall of Fame, former NFL coach Jon Gruden asked Desmond and fellow Class of 2011 inductee Dexter Coakley a few questions about their alma maters.

Desmond accepted a congratulatory handshake from fellow inductee and former University of Dayton head coach Mike Kelly after the pair received their College Football Hall of Fame blazers.

"When I think of Desmond, I think of his explosiveness and the different ways that he could hurt you as a receiver, as well as a returner. It's such a threat because you always have pressure on people, and he had a potential to hit a home run every time he touched the ball. He was a threat and when you can score on special teams — that's huge. Or just how he could change field-possession; He brought that as well as being a fine receiver. It's difficult to find someone like him."

BARRY ALVAREZ
Wisconsin Coach, 1990-2005
Class of 2011
College Football Hall of Fame

The Howard family cheers Desmond as he was officially inducted into the College Football Hall of Fame during the blazer presentation.

"He was an innovative football player at Michigan. He did things both acrobatically and athletically that kind of made people take a step back. When you have a standout, stand alone player like that, they come along maybe every 5-10 years. Finishing off the way he did with some of those big games on TV — that's what I remember most about Desmond, was reading about him and his feats. Without exception, when he hit the big stages he had the biggest performances."

RANDY CROSS
UCLA. Offensive Guard. 1973-75
Class of 2011
College Football Hall of Fame

"In athletics, you can't measure a guy's heart. To see him, he wasn't one of the biggest, yet he still ran across the middle and mixed it up. I watched his collegiate career, I watched his professional career, but you can't teach heart and courage. He had those things and he blossomed into a great player because of that. He's been to the pinnacle of every level that he's played, and that's saying something for a guy who's not the biggest, but he has that courage and he has heart."

DEXTER COAKLEY
Appalachian State. Linebacker. 1993-96
Class of 2011
College Football Hall of Fame

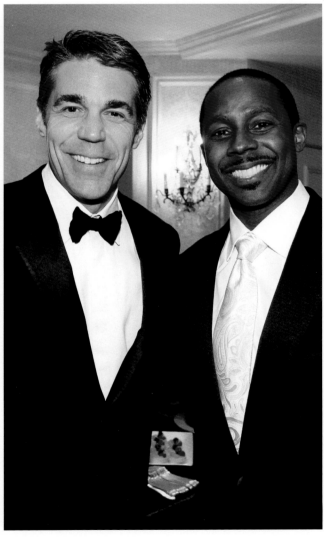

"If you asked anybody on our show, I don't think they would say that Desmond is pure character, a laugh-a-minute. He's got that side with that amazing laugh that can lift the whole room. But he's also got a very professional, reserved private side too. Behind that very charismatic smile, I think there is a very tough side to him. I think there's a very steely inside that goes along with that inherent shyness.

"He's increasingly become a strong voice for the players' perspective in the sport in terms of the issues that are in play. I don't hear too many analysts on TV — to be honest with you — champion some of these causes. I think analysts often see themselves as part of the establishment of the sport, therefore, they've become reluctant to criticize. And that is not Desmond. He does not see himself as part of the establishment; even tough he's a Heisman Trophy winner and a very prominent figure in college football history. I think he views himself as a champion of the players. I think he wisely stays in the periphery, as much as any Heisman winner and Hall of Famer can, he tends not to view himself as part of the inner-circle of the sport, and I think that's valuable."

CHRIS FOWLER (FAR LEFT)
ESPN
Host, College GameDay

9 STATISTICALLY SPEAKING

A comprehensive look back at Desmond's data

DESMOND'S CAREER TEAMMATES AT MICHIGAN

PLAYER	POS	HOMETOWN	GAMES*	PLAYER	POS	HOMETOWN	GAMES*
Erick Anderson	ILB	Glenview, IL	36	Marc Milia	C/OG	Birmingham, MI	12
J.D. Carlson	PK	Tallahassee, FL	36	Walter Smith	WR/DB	Detroit, MI	12
Joe Cocozzo	OG	Mechanicville, NY	36	Buster Stanley	DT	Youngstown, OH	12
Matt Elliott	OG/C	Carmel, IN	36	Mike Teeter	MG	Fruitport, MI	12
Mike Evans	DT	Roxbury, MA	36	Derrick Walker	TE	Glenwood, IL	12
Greg Skrepenak	OT	Wilkes Barre, PA	36	Marcus Walker	ILB	Chicago Heights, IL	12
Ken Sollom	PKH/QB	Canyon Country, CA	36	Brent White	DT	Dayton, OH	12
Brian Townsend	OLB	Cincinnati, OH	36	Chris Calloway	FLK	Chicago, IL	11
Lance Dottin	CB	Cambridge, MA	34	Dave Dobreff	ILB	Mt. Clemens, MI	11
Burnie Legette	FB	Colorado Springs, CO	34	Tony Henderson	MG	Indianapolis, IN	11
Alex Marshall	DT	Detroit, MI	34	Paul Manning	OG/C	Bloomfield Hills, MI	11
Elvis Grbac	QB	Willoughby Hills, OH	32	Steve Morrison	ILB	Birmingham, MI	11
Yale VanDyne	WR	Kearney, MO	32	Ninef Aghakhan	DT	Mt. Prospect, IL	10
Otis Williams	SS	Canton, OH	32	Tony Boles	RB	Westland, MI	10
Chris Hutchinson	DT	Houston, TX	31	Nate Holdren	ILB	Richland, WA	10
Corwin Brown	FS	Chicago, IL	31	Tyrone Wheatley	TB	Inkster, MI	10
David Ritter	SS	Hickory Hills, IL	30	Tim Williams	OLB	Milwaukee, WI	10
Dave Diebolt	TE	Mayfield, OH	28	Rusty Fichtner	LB	Meadville, PA	9
Rob Doherty	OT	Sterling Heights, MI	27	J.J. Grant	ILB	Liverpool, NY	9
Cornelius Simpson	OLB	Highland Park, MI	27	Deon Johnson	CB	Detroit, MI	9
Doug Skene	OG/OT	Fairview, TX	27	Felman Malveaux	WR	Beaumont, TX	9
Eduardo Azcona	P	Montreal, QUE	26	Greg McThomas	FB	Milwaukee, WI	9
Martin Davis	OLB	Chesapeake, VA	26	Bobby Powers	ILB	Kenner, LA	9
Coleman Wallace	CB	Willingboro, NJ	26	Eric Bush	FS	Quincy, IL	8
Dean Dingman	OG	East Troy, WI	24	John Ellison	WR	Delran, NJ	8
Tom Dohring	OT	Dearborn, MI	24	Michael Taylor	QB	Lincoln Heights, OH	8
Steve Everitt	C	Miami, FL	24	Matt Dyson	OLB	LaPlata, MD	7
David Key	DB	Columbus, OH	24	Marc Elliott	OLB	Carmel, IN	7
Tony McGee	TE	Terre Haute, IN	24	Todd Collins	PKH/QB	Walpole, MA	7
T.J. Osman	MG	Pittsburgh, PA	24	Eric Graves	MG	Akron, OH	7
Eric Traupe	ILB	Ashland, MA	24	Shawn Miller	OG	ElDorado, KS	7
Marc Burkholder	TE	Traverse City, MI	23	Shonte Peoples	DB	Saginaw, MI	7
Vada Murray	FS	Cincinnati, OH	23	Livetius Johnson	WR	Chicago, IL	6
Ricky Powers	TB	Akron, OH	23	Marc Spencer	LB	Troy, MI	6
Derrick Alexander	WR	Detroit, MI	22	John Albertson	PK	Portage, MI	5
Brian Wallace	OT	Parma, OH	22	Ron Buff	TB	Otisville, MI	5
Tripp Welborne	SS	Greensboro, NC	22	Barry Kelley	FB	Bolingbrook, IL	4
Todd Plate	DB	Brooklyn, MI	21	Doug Daugherty	OG	Romeo, MI	4
Jon Vaughn	TB	Florissant, MO	20	Kevin Owen	FLK	Moreland Hills, OH	4
Jarrod Bunch	FB	Ashtabula, OH	19	Tony Blankenship	DB	Detroit, MI	3
Curt Mallory	ILB	Bloomington, IN	19	Mike Nadlicki	FB	Traverse City, MI	3
Randy Stark	OLB	Mentor, OH	19	William Steuk	OLB	Sandusky, OH	2
Dwayne Ware	CB	Bloomington, IL	19	Shawn Watson	RB	Somerville, NJ	2
Allen Jefferson	TB	Detroit, MI	18	Paul Barry	OG	Cincinnati, OH	1
Dan Jokisch	TE/WR	Clarkston, MI	17	Jason Carr	QB	Ann Arbor, MI	1
John Milligan	ILB	Trenton, MI	17	Peter Elezovic	PK	Farmington Hills, MI	1
Alfie Burch	DB	Warren, OH	16	Curtis Feaster	LB	Flint, MI	1
Steve Rekowski	DT	Redford, MI	16	Che' Foster	FB	Edmond, OK	1
Chris Bohn	ILB	Traverse City, MI	14	Kevin Hedding	TE	Waterford, MI	1
Erik Knuth	MG	Plymouth, MI	14	John Jaeckin	TE	Cleveland, OH	1
Dennis Washington	TB	Lorain, OH	14	Gulam Khan	PK	Shaker Heights, OH	1
Pat Maloney	FS	LaGrange, IL	13	Joe Marinaro	OT	Andover, MA	1
Chris Stapleton	P	Springfield, IL	13	Leon Morton	DB	San Diego, CA	1
Bobby Abrams	OLB	Detroit, MI	12	Marc Ramirez	C/OG	Prairie View, IL	1
Gannon Dudlar	DL	Birmingham, MI	12	Jay Riemersma	QB	Zeeland, MI	1
Leroy Hoard	FB/TB	New Orleans, LA	12	Scott Smykowski	ILB	Sterling Heights, MI	1
Jesse Johnson	RB	Harper Woods, MI	12	John Woodlock	OG	Waynesburg, OH	1
Mike Maloney	OLB	Orland Park, IL	12	Steve Zacharias	TE	Sterling Heights, MI	1
Greg McMurtry	SE	Brockton, MA	12	Trent Zenkewicz	DL	Cleveland, OH	1

Actual Games Played Together

"When Desmond was playing at Michigan I was with the Minnesota Vikings. But if we weren't traveling, I was always watching the Michigan games. And I certainly saw that Ohio State game. That was outstanding, and something that I think shocked the world. It absolutely shocked me.

"But if you really looked at Des, he didn't look that fast. But once the ball was in the air, he had the tendencies to turn on the jets and a lot of times he laid out for a lot of balls. He was an outstanding football player. What can you say? You win the Heisman and you win MVP of the Super Bowl. There are only four guys who did both, and you can't take that away from him."

ANTHONY CARTER
Michigan
Wide Receiver, 1979-82; All-America, 1980-82
Class of 2001
College Football Hall of Fame

DESMOND'S CAREER STATISTICS VERSUS THE NCAA

RECEIVING

	GAMES	REC	YARDS	TD	LONG
Boston College	1	7	86	3	19
Florida State	1	4	69	2	42
Illinois	3	8	99	1	23
Indiana	3	17	211	4	36
Iowa	3	6	65	2	20
Maryland	2	3	59	1	37
Michigan State	3	16	241	2	29
Minnesota	3	15	260	4	65
Mississippi	1	6	167	2	63
Northwestern	1	4	102	1	64
Notre Dame	3	13	224	3	44
Ohio State	3	8	169	1	50
Purdue	3	13	191	4	47
UCLA	2	5	63	0	19
USC	1	0	0	0	0
Washington	1	1	35	0	35
Wisconsin	2	8	105	2	29
TOTALS	36	134	2,146	32	65

KICK RETURN

	GAMES	NUM	YARDS	TD	LONG
Boston College	1	1	93	1	93
Florida State	1	2	60	0	48
Illinois	3	5	132	0	43
Indiana	3	3	109	0	71
Iowa	3	3	96	0	42
Maryland	2	1	16	0	16
Michigan State	3	6	165	1	95
Minnesota	3	6	98	0	20
Mississippi	1	1	32	0	32
Northwestern	1	2	56	0	36
Notre Dame	3	5	143	0	41
Ohio State	3	2	51	0	35
Purdue	3	1	18	0	18
UCLA	2	3	78	0	38
USC	1	0	0	0	0
Washington	1	3	39	0	21
Wisconsin	2	1	25	0	25
TOTALS	36	45	1,211	2	95

RUSHING

	GAMES	ATT	YARDS	TD	LONG
Boston College	1	1	4	0	4
Florida State	1	0	0	0	0
Illinois	3	3	35	1	15
Indiana	3	1	17	0	17
Iowa	3	4	46	0	52
Maryland	2	1	6	0	6
Michigan State	3	1	4	0	4
Minnesota	3	2	41	0	26
Mississippi	1	1	19	0	19
Northwestern	1	1	18	0	19
Notre Dame	3	3	25	1	29
Ohio State	3	1	8	0	8
Purdue	3	2	21	0	13
UCLA	2	1	-10	0	0
USC	1	0	0	0	0
Washington	1	1	15	0	15
Wisconsin	2	0	0	0	0
TOTALS	36	23	249	2	52

PUNT RETURN

	GAMES	NUM	YARDS	TD	LONG
Boston College	1	3	3	0	3
Florida State	1	3	60	0	40
Illinois	3	0	0	0	0
Indiana	3	0	0	0	0
Iowa	3	2	1	0	4
Maryland	2	2	14	0	11
Michigan State	3	2	18	0	10
Minnesota	3	1	19	0	19
Mississippi	1	2	8	0	10
Northwestern	1	3	25	0	19
Notre Dame	3	1	8	0	8
Ohio State	3	2	107	1	93
Purdue	3	2	53	0	39
UCLA	2	0	0	0	0
USC	1	0	0	0	0
Washington	1	3	21	0	15
Wisconsin	2	0	0	0	0
TOTALS	36	26	337	1	93

"I remember recruiting Desmond back when I was an assistant at Michigan State and obviously he was an outstanding football player. The thing that stood out to me beyond all the athletic ability — even back then — was the kind of person Desmond was with a great smile and personality. You knew he was going to be successful in life because of that.

"There are a lot of really good athletes out there, but those that have the character and the drive like he did are the ones who are able to be great. It doesn't surprise me at all that Desmond has had success on every level playing football and now he's doing the same with his work on television. He's got to be right up there with the best players I wasn't able to sign and we still have a good time talking about the recruiting stories today."

NICK SABAN
Michigan State
Defensive Backs Coach, 1983-87

DESMOND'S COACHES AT MICHIGAN AND THE NFL

COACHES	TEAM	YEARS	COACHES	TEAM	YEARS	COACHES	TEAM	YEARS
* Gary Moeller	UM-DET	6	Kevin Higgins	DET	2	Lucious Selmon	JAX	1
Jason Arapoff	WAS-DET	5	Keith Rowen	OAK	2	Lionel Washington	GNB	1
Cam Cameron	UM -WAS	5	Johnny Holland	GNB	2	Larry Pasquale	JAX	1
Tom Reed	UM	4	Harry Sydney	GNB	2	Larry Brooks	GNB	1
Tirrel Burton	UM	4	Glenn Pires	DET	2	Larry Beightol	GNB	1
Lloyd Carr	UM	4	Garrett Glemont	OAK	2	Kurt Schottenheimer	DET	1
Les Miles	UM	4	Fred Biletnikoff	OAK	2	Kevin Spencer	OAK	1
Jim Herrmann	UM	4	Don Breaux	WAS	2	Kevin O'Dea	DET	1
Jerry Hanlon	UM	4	Dave Adolph	OAK	2	Kevin Gilbride	JAX	1
Emmitt Thomas	WAS-GNB	4	Charley Taylor	WAS	2	Kent Johnston	GNB	1
Don Clemons	DET	4	Charles Haley	DET	2	Ken Zampese	GNB	1
Dick Selcer	DET	4	Bobby DePaul	WAS	2	Keith Rowen	OAK	1
Chuck Priefer	DET	4	* Bobby Ross	DET	2	John Pease	JAX	1
Bobby Morrison	UM	4	* Bo Schembecher	UM	2	John Morton	OAK	1
Bill Harris	UM	4	Willie Shaw	OAK	1	John Marshall	DET	1
Sherman Lewis	GNB-DET	3	Tom Lovat	GNB	1	Joe Vitt	GNB	1
Russ Grimm	WAS	3	Terry Robiskie	WAS	1	Joe Baker	JAX	1
Jim Hanifan	WAS	3	Steve Szabo	JAX	1	Jim Lind	GNB	1
Dan Riley	WAS	3	Steve Ortmayer	GNB	1	Jerry Palmieri	JAX	1
* Marty Mornhinweg	GNB-DET	3	Skip Peete	OAK	1	Jerald Ingram	JAX	1
Willie Borwn	OAK	2	Ron Lynn	WAS	1	Jeff Jagodzinski	GNB	1
Wayne Sevier	WAS	2	Ray Perkins	OAK	1	Jeff Hurd	JAX	1
Torgy Torgeson	WAS	2	Randy Edsall	JAX	1	Irv Eatman	GNB	1
TJ Weist	UM	2	Phil Bromley	UM	1	Gil Haskell	GNB	1
Sean Kugler	DET	2	Pete Rodriguez	WAS	1	Gary Stevens	OAK	1
Rod Dowhower	WAS	2	Pete Carmichael	JAX	1	Fritz Shurmur	GNB	1
Robert Jenkins	OAK	2	Nolan Cromwell	GNB	1	Frank Gansz, Jr.	OAK	1
Rennie Simmons	WAS	2	Nick Nicolau	JAX	1	Don Martin	OAK	1
Ray Horton	WAS-DET	2	Mike Waufle	OAK	1	Dick Jauron	JAX	1
Mike McHugh	DET	2	Mike Trgovac	GNB	1	David Shaw	OAK	1
Maurice Carthon	DET	2	Mike McCarthy	GNB	1	Chuck Knox, Jr.	GNB	1
Malcolm Blacken	DET	2	Mike Maser	JAX	1	Chuck Bresnahan	OAK	1
Larry Kirksey	DET	2	Mike Haluchak	WAS	1	Charlie Baggett	GNB	1
						Bobby Jackson	WAS	1
						Bob Valesente	GNB	1
						Bob Karmelowicz	WAS	1
						Bill Musgrave	OAK	1
						Bill Callahan	OAK	1
						Barry Rubin	GNB	1
						Andy Reid	GNB	1
						* Tom Coughlin	JAX	1
						* Richie Petitbon	WAS	1
						* Ray Rhodes	GNB	1
						* Norv Turner	WAS	1
						* Mike Holmgren	GNB	1
						* Jon Gruden	OAK	1
						* Joe Gibbs	WAS	1
						* Joe Bugel	OAK	1

Desmond with his former UM receivers coach T.J. Weist

* *Head Coaches*

"Desmond was the toughest guy I played against in 1991, because here was a guy who could run routes. But the thing that separated him from other great receivers was that Desmond could finish. He had that big old offensive line and he would run deeper routes and put pressure on you. When that ball was in the air, he was going to go get it.

"I remember he ran a post-corner route on me in the back of the end zone. I thought I had a beat on him, and I go to jump for the interception, but Desmond had this kind of lean where he put that leg out when he jumped. I was trying to go up and that leg impeded me, and I landed on my shoulder pad. And this guy still makes the catch, falls into the goal post and holds on to the ball. ... That's the type of player that you were dealing with. That's what you get with a Heisman winner."

TERRELL BUCKLEY
Florida State
Cornerback, 1989-91; All-America, 1991

DESMOND'S CAREER TEAMMATES IN THE NFL

PLAYER	POS	TEAMS	GAMES*	PLAYER	POS	TEAMS	GAMES*	PLAYER	POS	TEAMS	GAMES*
Raleigh McKenzie	OL	WAS-GNB	56	James Jett	WR	OAK	30	Germane Crowell	WR	DET	22
Ray Brown	OL	WAS-DET	55	Lincoln Kennedy	OT	OAK	30	Earl Dotson	OT	GNB	22
Kelvin Pritchett	DT	JAX-DET	53	Barret Robbins	C	OAK	30	Herman Moore	WR	DET	22
Chip Lohmiller	K	WAS	48	Darrell Russell	DL	OAK	30	Olanda Truitt	WR	WAS-OAK	22
Brian Mitchell	RB	WAS	48	Sterling Palmer	DE	WAS	30	Bradford Banta	TE	DET	21
Ricky Ervins	RB	WAS	47	James Trapp	SS	OAK	30	Todd Lyght	CB	DET	21
Kurt Gouveia	LB	WAS	46	Adam Treu	C	OAK	30	Stockar McDougle	OT	DET	21
Lamont Hollinquest	LB	WAS-GNB	46	Steve Wisniewski	OG	OAK	30	Dominic Raiola	C	DET	21
Johnny Thomas	DB	WAS	46	Guy Bingham	OL	WAS	29	Eric Turner	FS	OAK	21
Monte Coleman	LB	WAS	45	Jason Buck	DT	WAS	29	Bruce Wilkerson	OL	JAX-GNB	21
Tim Johnson	DT	WAS	45	Russell Maryland	DT	WAS	29	Jeff Bostic	C	WAS	20
Ed Simmons	OL	WAS	45	Brock Olivo	RB	DET	29	Calvin Branch	DB	OAK	20
Andre Collins	LB	WAS	43	Kenny Shedd	WR	OAK	29	Barrett Brooks	OT	DET	20
Chris Claiborne	LB	DET	41	Harvey Williams	RB	OAK	29	Perry Carter	CB	OAK	20
Jason Hanson	K	DET	41	Reggie Brooks	RB	WAS	28	Mike Compton	C	DET	20
Robert Porcher	DE	DET	41	Pat Eilers	DB	WAS	28	Santana Dotson	DL	GNB	20
Mark Schlereth	OT	WAS	41	Barrett Green	LB	DET	28	Mo Elewonibi	OT	WAS	20
Cory Schlesinger	FB	DET	41	Lance Johnstone	DE	OAK	28	Antonio Freeman	WR	GNB	20
Eric Beverly	OL	DET	40	Charles Mann	DE	WAS	28	Pat Harlow	OT	OAK	20
Darrell Green	CB	WAS	40	Mark Rypien	QB	WAS	28	Jeff Hartings	C	DET	20
James Stewart	RB	JAX-DET	40	Danny Copeland	SS	WAS	27	James Jones	DT	DET	20
John Jett	P	DET	39	Napoleon Kaufman	RB	OAK	27	Matt Joyce	OT	DET	20
Luther Elliss	DL	DET	38	Albert Lewis	CB	OAK	27	John Henry Mills	LB	OAK	20
A.J. Johnson	CB	WAS	38	Jimmy Wyrick	DB	DET	27	Darryl Morrison	FS	WAS	20
Travis Kirschke	DE	DET	37	Todd Bowles	FS	WAS	26	Terry Orr	TE	WAS	20
James Jenkins	TE	WAS	36	Mike Morton	LB	OAK	26	Walter Rasby	TE	DET	20
Lamar Campbell	DB	DET	35	Ron Rice	SS	DET	26	Shaun Rogers	DT	DET	19
Tony Semple	OG	DET	35	Marquis Walker	CB	OAK-DET	26	Kurt Schulz	FS	DET	19
Allen Aldridge	LB	DET	34	Bobby Wilson	DT	WAS	26	Stephen Trejo	FB	DET	19
Johnnie Morton	WR	DET	34	Charlie Batch	QB	DET	25	Corwin Brown	SS	DET	18
Tracy Scroggins	LB	DET	34	Larry Foster	WR	DET	25	Rick Cunningham	OT	OAK	18
Scott Kowalkowski	LB	DET	33	James Hall	DE	DET	25	Grady Jackson	DT	OAK	18
Alvoid Mays	DB	WAS	33	Bryant Westbrook	CB	DET	25	Joe Jacoby	OT	WAS	18
David Sloan	TE	DET	33	Kerlin Blaise	OG	DET	24	Keith McKenzie	DE	GNB	18
Leo Araguz	P	OAK-DET	32	LeRoy Butler	SS	GNB	24	Pete Mitchell	TE	JAX-DET	18
Earnest Byner	RB	WAS	32	Terry Fair	CB	DET	24	Brian Stablein	WR	DET	18
Jared DeVries	DE	DET	32	Brett Favre	QB	GNB	24	Frank Wycheck	TE	WAS	18
Brad Edwards	DB	WAS	32	Bernardo Harris	LB	GNB	24	Kelly Goodburn	P	WAS	17
Ron Middleton	TE	WAS	32	William Henderson	FB	GNB	24	Rick Hamilton	LB	WAS	17
Art Monk	WR	WAS	32	Randy Jordan	RB	JAX-OAK	24	Martin Bayless	SS	WAS	16
Clint Kriewaldt	LB	DET	31	George Koonce	LB	GNB	24	Don Beebe	WR	GNB	16
Reggie Roby	P	WAS	31	Dorsey Levens	RB	GNB	24	Edgar Bennett	RB	GNB	16
Ricky Sanders	WR	WAS	31	Jeff Thomason	TE	GNB	24	Gary Clark	WR	WAS	16
Brian M. Williams	LB	GNB-DET	31	Tyrone Williams	CB	GNB	24	Ron Cox	LB	GNB	16
Greg Biekert	LB	OAK	30	Frank Winters	C	GNB	24	Henry Ellard	WR	WAS	16
Tim Brown	WR	OAK	30	Stephen Boyd	LB	DET	23	Matt Elliott	OL	WAS	16
Tom Carter	CB	WAS	30	Jeff George	QB	OAK	23	Doug Evans	CB	GNB	16
Shane Collins	DE	WAS	30	Jim Lachey	OT	WAS	23	John Friesz	QB	WAS	16
Rickey Dudley	TE	OAK	30	Terry Mickens	WR	GNB-OAK	23	Jumpy Geathers	DL	WAS	16
James Folston	LB	OAK	30	Jeff Backus	OT	DET	22	Aaron Gibson	OT	DET	16

*Actual Games Played Together

"I have one thing in common with Desmond Howard: we both wore the same number. ...
But his collegiate career at the University of Michigan — now, I'm a football fan — so I
follow Michigan, and I certainly followed his career; and as you look at his professional
success, here is a guy who has been clean all of his life and has never gotten into trouble.
So he is a real asset to sports, and not only the University of Michigan, but the state of
Michigan."

DAVE BING
Mayor of Detroit
Detroit Pistons Guard, 1966-78
Naismith Basketball Hall of Fame, 1990

DESMOND'S CAREER TEAMMATES IN THE NFL

PLAYER	POS	TEAMS	GAMES*	PLAYER	POS	TEAMS	GAMES*	PLAYER	POS	TEAMS	GAMES*
Ken Harvey	LB	WAS	16	Deral Boykin	DB	WAS-JAX	14	Tom McManus	LB	JAX	11
Craig Hentrich	P	GNB	16	Lester Holmes	OG	OAK	14	Heath Shuler	QB	WAS	11
Darius Holland	DT	GNB	16	Kevin L. Johnson	DT	OAK	14	Don Warren	TE	WAS	11
Ethan Horton	TE	WAS	16	Tre Johnson	OG	WAS	14	Eric Allen	CB	OAK	10
Chris Jacke	K	GNB	16	Lorenzo Lynch	SS	OAK	14	Eddie Anderson	FS	OAK	10
Keith Jackson	TE	GNB	16	Roderick Mullen	DB	GNB	14	Tony Boselli	OT	JAX	10
Travis Jervey	RB	GNB	16	Louis Riddick	DB	OAK	14	Aundray Bruce	LB	OAK	10
Leonard Marshall	DT	WAS	16	Jon Ritchie	FB	OAK	14	Mark Brunell	QB	JAX	10
Wilber Marshall	LB	WAS	16	Bill Schroeder	WR	GNB-DET	14	Ryan Christopherson	RB	JAX	10
Trevor Matich	OL	WAS	16	Bryan Schwartz	LB	JAX	14	Martin Mayhew	CB	WAS	10
Craig Newsome	CB	GNB	16	Cedric Smith	FB	WAS	14	Anthony Newman	SS	OAK	10
Al Noga	DE	WAS	16	Brenden Stai	OG	DET	14	Santo Stephens	LB	JAX	10
Mike Prior	FS	GNB	16	Curtis Whitley	C	OAK	14	Cedric Tillman	WR	JAX	10
Eugene Robinson	FS	GNB	16	Robert Bailey	CB	DET	13	Darnell Walker	CB	DET	10
Jeff Rutledge	QB	WAS	16	Bryan Barker	P	JAX	13	Eric Williams	DT	WAS	10
Wayne Simmons	LB	GNB	16	Vinnie Clark	CB	JAX	13	Marc Boutte	DT	WAS	9
Fred Stokes	DE	WAS	16	Harry Colon	SS	JAX	13	Eugene Chung	OG	JAX	9
Tyronne Stowe	LB	WAS	16	Don Davey	DT	JAX	13	Corey Dowden	DB	GNB	9
Aaron Taylor	OG	GNB	16	Brian DeMarco	OL	JAX	13	Derrick Fenner	RB	OAK	9
Adam Timmerman	OG	GNB	16	Keith Goganious	LB	JAX	13	Ray Hall	DT	JAX	9
Lamont Warren	RB	DET	16	Alan Grant	DB	WAS	13	Sedrick Irvin	RB	DET	9
Mickey Washington	CB	JAX	16	Rich Griffith	TE	JAX	13	Lindsay Knapp	OG	GNB	9
Reggie White	DE	GNB	16	Mike Hollis	K	JAX	13	Chad Levitt	RB	OAK	9
Gabe Wilkins	DL	GNB	16	Le'Shai Maston	FB	JAX	13	Khari Samuel	LB	DET	9
Carl Banks	LB	WAS	15	Corey Mayfield	DT	JAX	13	Lionel Washington	CB	OAK	9
Derek V. Brown	TE	OAK	15	Tim McGee	WR	WAS	13	James E. Williams	LB	JAX	9
Mark Chmura	TE	GNB	15	Lamar Mills	DE	WAS	13	Jermaine Williams	RB	OAK	9
Mo Collins	OT	OAK	15	Jeff Novak	OG	JAX	13	Tony Barker	LB	WAS	8
Greg Davis	K	OAK	15	Ray Roberts	OT	DET	13	William Bell	RB	WAS	8
Cole Ford	K	OAK	15	Anthony Smith	DE	OAK	13	Vaughn Booker	DE	GNB	8
Rob Fredrickson	LB	OAK	15	Jimmy Smith	WR	JAX	13	Corey Bradford	WR	GNB	8
John Gesek	C	WAS	15	Dave Thomas	CB	JAX	13	Gary L. Brown	OT	GNB	8
Robert Green	DB	WAS	15	Dave Widell	C	JAX	13	Gilbert Brown	DT	GNB	8
Tim Hall	RB	OAK	15	Jim Wahler	NT	WAS	13	Shannon Clavelle	DE	GNB	8
James Harris	DE	OAK	15	Mario Bates	RB	DET	12	Anthony Davis	LB	GNB	8
Richard Harvey	LB	OAK	15	John Brantley	LB	WAS	12	Rob Davis	C	GNB	8
Rob Holmberg	LB	OAK	15	Greg Huntington	OL	JAX	12	Tyrone Davis	TE	GNB	8
Sean Jones	DE	GNB	15	Ernie Logan	DT	JAX	12	Antuan Edwards	SS	GNB	8
Dan Land	DB	OAK	15	Terry McDaniel	CB	OAK	12	Bert Emanuel	WR	DET	8
Chester McGlockton	DT	OAK	15	Kevin O'Neill	LB	DET	12	Gus Frerotte	QB	WAS-DET	8
John Michels	OT	GNB	15	Vernice Smith	OG	JAX	12	Rich Gannon	QB	WAS	8
Dexter Nottage	DE	WAS	15	Kywin Supernaw	DB	DET	12	Matt Hasselbeck	QB	GNB	8
Joel Smeenge	DE	JAX	15	Aveion Cason	RB	DET	11	Vonnie Holliday	DE	GNB	8
Pat Swilling	DE	OAK	15	Mike Dumas	FS	JAX	11	Sidney Johnson	DB	WAS	8
Tydus Winans	WR	WAS	15	Vaughn Dunbar	RB	JAX	11	Craig Keith	TE	JAX	8
Terry Wooden	LB	WAS	15	Derrick Graham	OG	OAK	11	Jeff Lageman	DE	JAX	8
Tony Woods	DE	WAS	15	Rogerick Green	DB	JAX	11	Ryan Longwell	K	GNB	8
Charles Woodson	CB	OAK	15	Donald Hollas	QB	OAK	11	Billy Lyon	DL	GNB	8
Scotty Anderson	WR	DET	14	Chidi Iwuoma	DB	DET	11	Scott McGarrahan	DB	GNB	8
Darryl Ashmore	OT	OAK	14	Willie Jackson	WR	JAX	11	Gene McGuire	C	GNB	8

Actual Games Played Together

DESMOND'S CAREER TEAMMATES IN THE NFL

PLAYER	POS	TEAMS	GAMES*	PLAYER	POS	TEAMS	GAMES*	PLAYER	POS	TEAMS	GAMES*
Mike McKenzie	CB	GNB	8	Mike Arthur	C	GNB	5	Mark Stock	WR	WAS	3
Mike McMahon	QB	DET	8	J.B. Brown	CB	DET	5	Josh Thornhill	LB	DET	3
Basil Mitchell	RB	GNB	8	Mark Carrier	FS	DET	5	Erick Anderson	LB	WAS	2
Jim Nelson	LB	GNB	8	Bernard Carter	LB	JAX	5	James Atkins	OT	DET	2
Alfred Pupunu	TE	DET	8	Reggie Clark	LB	JAX	5	Brant Boyer	LB	JAX	2
Marco Rivera	OG	GNB	8	Eric Davis	FS	DET	5	Jeremy Brigham	TE	OAK	2
Darren Sharper	FS	GNB	8	Antonio Dingle	DT	GNB	5	Gregory Clifton	WR	WAS	2
Darren Studstill	DB	JAX	8	Jeff Faulkner	DL	WAS	5	Chris Hayes	DB	GNB	2
Ross Verba	OT	GNB	8	Andre' Goodman	CB	DET	5	Stephen Hobbs	WR	WAS	2
Fred Vinson	DB	GNB	8	Rick Graf	LB	WAS	5	Richard Huntley	RB	DET	2
Mike Wahle	OL	GNB	8	Jim McMahon	QB	GNB	5	Charles Jordan	WR	GNB	2
Aaron Wallace	LB	OAK	8	Dan Owens	DT	DET	5	Antwan Lake	DE	DET	2
Mark Williams	LB	JAX	8	Tony Ramirez	OT	DET	5	Gordon Laro	TE	JAX	2
Louie Aguiar	P	GNB	7	Andre Rison	WR	GNB	5	Johnny Meads	LB	WAS	2
Joe Andruzzi	OG	GNB	7	Tyrone Rush	RB	WAS	5	Darryl Moore	OG	WAS	2
Steve Beuerlein	QB	JAX	7	Alonzo Spellman	DL	DET	5	Matt Murphy	TE	DET	2
Shawn Bouwens	OG	JAX	7	Larry Brown	CB	OAK	4	Gerald Nichols	DT	WAS	2
Bucky Brooks	WR	GNB-OAK	7	Ravin Caldwell	LB	WAS	4	Joe Patton	OT	WAS	2
Robert Brooks	WR	GNB	7	Marty Carter	SS	DET	4	Marc Raab	C	WAS	2
Chris Cash	CB	DET	7	Stoney Case	QB	DET	4	Jim Riggs	TE	WAS	2
Ben Coleman	OG	JAX	7	Ty Detmer	QB	DET	4	Juan Roque	OT	DET	2
Donte Curry	LB	DET	7	Monty Grow	DB	JAX	4	Ashley Sheppard	LB	JAX	2
Travis Davis	SS	JAX	7	David Gulledge	DB	WAS	4	Travian Smith	LB	OAK	2
Jerone Davison	RB	OAK	7	Greg Hill	RB	DET	4	Mike Thompson	DT	JAX	2
Reuben Droughns	RB	DET	7	Cletidus Hunt	DT	GNB	4	Jahine Arnold	WR	GNB	1
Kalimba Edwards	DE	DET	7	Ray McElroy	SS	DET	4	Rodney Artmore	DB	GNB	1
Mike Flanagan	OL	GNB	7	De'Mond Parker	RB	GNB	4	John Brandes	TE	WAS	1
Paul Frase	DE	JAX	7	Anthony Prior	DB	OAK	4	Pete Chryplewicz	TE	DET	1
Ernest Givins	WR	JAX	7	Travis Reece	RB	DET	4	Reggie Cobb	RB	JAX	1
Jeff Gooch	LB	DET	7	Huey Richardson	LB	WAS	4	Eddie Drummond	WR	DET	1
Mike Haight	OG	WAS	7	Ray Rowe	TE	WAS	4	Chris Hanson	P	GNB	1
Az-Zahir Hakim	WR	DET	7	Ken Ruettgers	OT	GNB	4	Carl Harry	WR	WAS	1
Joey Harrington	QB	DET	7	Matt Snider	FB	GNB	4	Anthony Herron	DE	DET	1
Corey Harris	SS	DET	7	Tyree Talton	DB	DET	4	Tyrone Hopson	OG	DET	1
Curtis Marsh	WR	JAX	7	Greg Townsend	DL	OAK	4	Chris Hudson	FS	JAX	1
Derrick Mayes	WR	GNB	7	Brian Walker	FS	DET	4	Rob Johnson	QB	JAX	1
Tod McBride	CB	GNB	7	Wade Wilson	QB	DET	4	Tommy Johnson	DB	JAX	1
Tom Myslinski	OG	WAS-JAX	7	Vince Amey	DE	OAK	3	Calvin Jones	RB	GNB	1
John Owens	TE	DET	7	Cary Conklin	QB	WAS	3	Richard Jordan	LB	DET	1
Jermaine Smith	DT	GNB	7	Frank Cornish	OL	JAX	3	David Klingler	QB	OAK	1
Bracy Walker	SS	DET	7	Jeff Dellenbach	C	GNB	3	Bob Kuberski	DT	GNB	1
Joe Aska	RB	OAK	6	Andre Dixon	DB	DET	3	Doug Pederson	QB	GNB	1
Tommy Bennett	SS	DET	6	Ernest Dixon	LB	OAK	3	Ron Rivers	RB	DET	1
Darren Carrington	SS	JAX	6	Dwayne Harper	CB	DET	3	Brian Satterfield	RB	GNB	1
Lamont Hall	TE	GNB	6	Jeremy Lincoln	CB	DET	3	Sebastian Savage	RB	WAS	1
Kurt Haws	TE	WAS	6	Bronzell Miller	DE	JAX	3	Kevin Smith	TE	GNB	1
Chuck Osborne	DT	OAK	6	Anthony Morgan	WR	GNB	3	Ryan Stewart	DB	DET	1
Mikhael Ricks	TE	DET	6	Bob Rosenstiel	DE	OAK	3	Keith Taylor	DB	WAS	1
Mike Robinson	DB	GNB	6	Leslie Shepherd	WR	WAS	3	Iheanyi Uwaezuoke	WR	DET	1
Jude Waddy	LB	GNB	6	Ed Smith	TE	DET	3	Keith Willis	DE	WAS	1

Actual Games Played Together

DESMOND'S CAREER PLAYOFF TEAMMATES IN THE NFL

PLAYER	POS	COLLEGE	GAMES	PLAYER	POS	COLLEGE	GAMES	PLAYER	POS	COLLEGE	GAMES
Don Beebe	WR	Western Illinois	3	William Henderson	FB	North Carolina	3	Andre Rison	WR	Michigan State	3
Edgar Bennett	RB	Florida State	3	Craig Hentrich	P	Notre Dame	3	Eugene Robinson	FS	Colgate	3
Gary L. Brown	OT	Georgia Tech	3	Darius Holland	DT	Colorado	3	Wayne Simmons	LB	Clemson	3
Gilbert Brown	DT	Kansas	3	Lamont Hollinquest	LB	USC	3	Aaron Taylor	OG	Notre Dame	3
LeRoy Butler	SS	Florida State	3	Chris Jacke	PK	Texas-El Paso	3	Jeff Thomason	TE	Oregon	3
Mark Chmura	TE	Boston College	3	Keith Jackson	TE	Oklahoma	3	Adam Timmerman	OG	South Dakota State	3
Ron Cox	LB	Fresno State	3	Travis Jervey	RB	Citadel	3	Reggie White	DE	Tennessee	3
Jeff Dellenbach	OL	Wisconsin	3	Sean Jones	DE	Northeastern	3	Bruce Wilkerson	OT	Tennessee	3
Earl Dotson	OT	Texas A&M-Kingsville	3	Lindsay Knapp	OG	Notre Dame	3	Gabe Wilkins	DT	Gardner-Webb	3
Santana Dotson	DT	Baylor	3	Keith McKenzie	DE	Ball State	3	Brian M. Williams	LB	USC	3
Doug Evans	CB	Louisiana Tech	3	John Michels	OT	USC	3	Tyrone Williams	CB	Nebraska	3
Brett Favre	QB	So. Mississippi	3	Terry Mickens	WR	Florida A&M	3	Frank Winters	C	Western Illinois	3
Antonio Freeman	WR	Virginia Tech	3	Roderick Mullen	DB	Grambling State	3	Calvin Jones	RB	Nebraska	2
Bernardo Harris	LB	North Carolina	3	Craig Newsome	CB	Arizona State	3	Jim McMahon	QB	BYU	2
Chris Hayes	DB	Washington State	3	Mike Prior	FS	Illinois State	3	George Koonce	LB	East Carolina	1

DESMOND'S CAREER STATISTICS VERSUS THE NFL

RECEIVING

	GAMES	REC	YARDS	TD	LONG
Arizona Cardinals	7	6	94	0	25
Atlanta Falcons	5	4	69	0	25
Baltimore Ravens	1	0	0	0	0
Buffalo Bills	3	2	38	0	27
Carolina Panthers	3	2	14	0	7
Chicago Bears	8	3	27	0	14
Cincinnati Bengals	4	7	88	0	23
Cleveland Browns	2	1	24	0	24
Dallas Cowboys	7	9	126	1	20
Denver Broncos	9	4	42	0	16
Detroit Lions	5	5	35	0	12
Green Bay Packers	5	5	46	0	13
Houston Oilers	2	6	65	1	15
Indianapolis Colts	4	3	18	0	6
Jacksonville Jaguars	1	0	0	0	0
Kansas City Chiefs	6	1	10	0	10
LA/Oakland Raiders	2	1	7	0	7
Los Angeles Rams	2	3	64	0	39
Miami Dolphins	3	1	9	0	9
Minnesota Vikings	11	9	98	0	20
New England Patriots	1	0	0	0	0
New Orleans Saints	5	3	45	1	31
New York Giants	8	11	165	0	27
New York Jets	4	3	38	0	15
Philadelphia Eagles	7	7	102	1	28
Pittsburgh Steelers	2	0	0	0	0
San Diego Chargers	5	0	0	0	0
San Francisco 49ers	3	7	62	0	12
Seattle Seahawks	8	3	35	1	27
St. Louis Rams	3	0	0	0	0
Tampa Bay Buccaneers	12	16	240	1	81
Tennessee Titans	2	1	36	1	36
Washington Redskins	3	0	0	0	0
TOTALS	**153**	**123**	**1,597**	**7**	**81**

RUSHING

	GAMES	ATT	YARDS	TD	LONG
Arizona Cardinals	7	1	2	0	2
Atlanta Falcons	5	0	0	0	0
Baltimore Ravens	1	0	0	0	0
Buffalo Bills	3	0	0	0	0
Carolina Panthers	3	0	0	0	0
Chicago Bears	8	1	5	0	5
Cincinnati Bengals	4	1	8	0	8
Cleveland Browns	2	0	0	0	0
Dallas Cowboys	7	0	0	0	0
Denver Broncos	9	0	0	0	0
Detroit Lions	5	0	0	0	0
Green Bay Packers	5	0	0	0	0
Houston Oilers	2	0	0	0	0
Indianapolis Colts	4	0	0	0	0
Jacksonville Jaguars	1	0	0	0	0
Kansas City Chiefs	6	0	0	0	0
LA/Oakland Raiders	2	0	0	0	0
Los Angeles Rams	2	0	0	0	0
Miami Dolphins	3	2	17	0	9
Minnesota Vikings	11	0	0	0	0
New England Patriots	1	0	0	0	0
New Orleans Saints	5	1	7	0	7
New York Giants	8	1	5	0	5
New York Jets	4	0	0	0	0
Philadelphia Eagles	7	0	0	0	0
Pittsburgh Steelers	2	0	0	0	0
San Diego Chargers	5	0	0	0	0
San Francisco 49ers	3	0	0	0	0
Seattle Seahawks	8	0	0	0	0
St. Louis Rams	3	2	11	0	7
Tampa Bay Buccaneers	12	2	10	0	6
Tennessee Titans	2	1	3	0	3
Washington Redskins	3	0	0	0	0
TOTALS	**153**	**12**	**68**	**0**	**9**

DESMOND'S CAREER STATISTICS VERSUS THE NFL

KICK RETURN

	GAMES	NUM	YARDS	TD	LONG
Arizona Cardinals	7	12	245	0	32
Atlanta Falcons	5	8	202	0	25
Baltimore Ravens	1	2	37	0	20
Buffalo Bills	3	11	208	0	33
Carolina Panthers	3	7	148	0	18
Chicago Bears	8	21	449	0	37
Cincinnati Bengals	4	7	271	0	91
Cleveland Browns	2	9	196	0	37
Dallas Cowboys	7	18	333	0	20
Denver Broncos	9	36	674	0	29
Detroit Lions	5	5	101	0	27
Green Bay Packers	5	23	523	0	36
Houston Oilers	2	0	0	0	0
Indianapolis Colts	4	6	154	0	33
Jacksonville Jaguars	1	4	74	0	19
Kansas City Chiefs	6	25	508	0	42
LA/Oakland Raiders	2	1	20	0	20
Los Angeles Rams	2	0	0	0	0
Miami Dolphins	3	7	123	0	20
Minnesota Vikings	11	27	543	0	40
New England Patriots	1	4	136	0	45
New Orleans Saints	5	8	192	0	70
New York Giants	8	9	206	0	42
New York Jets	4	10	213	0	27
Philadelphia Eagles	7	5	87	0	18
Pittsburgh Steelers	2	8	182	0	28
San Diego Chargers	5	15	365	0	39
San Francisco 49ers	3	3	73	0	33
Seattle Seahawks	8	19	442	0	35
St. Louis Rams	3	7	145	0	29
Tampa Bay Buccaneers	12	28	701	0	70
Tennessee Titans	2	4	184	0	59
Washington Redskins	3	10	224	0	44
TOTALS	153	359	7,959	0	91

PUNT RETURN

	GAMES	NUM	YARDS	TD	LONG
Arizona Cardinals	7	5	90	0	43
Atlanta Falcons	5	5	68	1	55
Baltimore Ravens	1	1	0	0	0
Buffalo Bills	3	4	112	1	75
Carolina Panthers	3	4	51	0	11
Chicago Bears	8	8	133	1	75
Cincinnati Bengals	4	9	63	0	18
Cleveland Browns	2	3	8	0	5
Dallas Cowboys	7	9	44	0	8
Denver Broncos	9	16	119	0	22
Detroit Lions	5	12	238	1	12
Green Bay Packers	5	12	143	0	30
Houston Oilers	2	5	45	0	11
Indianapolis Colts	4	4	94	0	80
Jacksonville Jaguars	1	0	0	0	0
Kansas City Chiefs	6	13	88	0	12
LA/Oakland Raiders	2	2	20	0	13
Los Angeles Rams	2	0	0	0	0
Miami Dolphins	3	3	15	0	13
Minnesota Vikings	11	23	288	0	34
New England Patriots	1	2	22	0	17
New Orleans Saints	5	9	180	1	95
New York Giants	8	4	77	0	50
New York Jets	4	5	65	0	15
Philadelphia Eagles	7	6	25	0	5
Pittsburgh Steelers	2	2	20	0	10
San Diego Chargers	5	22	246	1	23
San Francisco 49ers	3	6	28	0	7
Seattle Seahawks	8	19	254	1	63
St. Louis Rams	3	6	80	0	18
Tampa Bay Buccaneers	12	17	176	0	17
Tennessee Titans	2	3	9	0	2
Washington Redskins	3	5	94	1	68
TOTALS	153	244	2,895	8	95

DESMOND'S CAREER TOUCHDOWNS BY STADIUMS

STADIUM	HOST	LOCATION	TD
Michigan Stadium	University of Michigan	Ann Arbor, MI	15
Alumni Stadium	Boston College	Chestnut Hill, MA	4
Metrodome	University of Minnesota	Minneapolis, MN	3
RFK Stadium	Washington Redskins	Washington, D.C.	3
Superdome	New Orleans Saints/Super Bowl XXXI	New Orleans, LA	3
Silverdome	Detroit Lions	Pontiac, MI	3
Lambeau Field	Green Bay Packers	Green Bay, WI	3
Notre Dame Stadium	University of Notre Dame	South Bend, IN	2
Camp Randall Stadium	Univeristy of Wisconsin	Madison, WI	2
Gator Bowl Stadium	Jacksonville Jaguars	Jacksonville, FL	2
Kinnick Stadium	University of Iowa	Iowa City, IA	2
Spartan Stadium	Michigan State University	East Lansing, MI	2
Memorial Stadium	University of Illinois	Champaign, IL	2
Memorial Stadium	University of Indiana	Bloomington, IN	1
Ross Ade Stadium	Purdue University	West Lafayette, IN	1
Ohio Stadium	Ohio State University	Columbus, OH	1
Texas Stadium	Dallas Cowboys	Irving, TX	1
Tampa Stadium	Tampa Bay Buccaneers	Tampa, FL	1
Astrodome	Houston Oilers	Houston, TX	1
Oakland-Alameda County Coliseum	Oakland Raiders	Oakland, CA	1
Rich Stadium	Buffalo Bills	Orchard Park, NY	1

THE TIMELINE OF DESMOND'S CAREER

1988

Feb. 10 – Signed a letter of intent to attend the University of Michigan.

1989

Nov. 4 – Scored first touchdown as a Wolverine, on an eight-yard pass from Michael Taylor during a 42-27 victory over Purdue.

1990

Sept. 15 – Enjoyed first multi-TD game at Michigan, catching two touchdown passes from Elvis Grbac during a 28-24 loss to Notre Dame.

Oct. 6 – Caught a pair of TD passes in a 41-3 victory over Wisconsin.

Oct. 13 – Scored his first return TD as a Wolverine, running back a kickoff 95 yards during a 28-27 loss to Michigan State.

Nov. 24 - Finished season with 29.5 yard per kick return, second overall in NCAA behind Tennessee's Dale Carter. Set a Michigan record with an average of 24.3 in overall return yardage.

1991

Jan. 1 – In his bowl game debut, caught two scoring passes from Grbac during a 35-3 rout of Mississippi in the Gator Bowl. His 167 receiving yards set a Michigan bowl record.

Sept. 7 – Scored four touchdowns, one shy of the Michigan single-game record, in a season-opening 35-13 win at Boston College. Tied the Michigan single-game mark with three TD receptions.

Sept. 14 – Caught two TD passes to lead Michigan to a 24-14 win over Notre Dame, ending the Wolverines' four-game losing streak against the Fighting Irish.

Sept. 28 – Caught two TD passes in Michigan's 51-31 loss to Florida State.

Oct. 5 – Caught two TD passes in a 51-31 win at Iowa.

Oct. 12 – Caught two TD passes as Michigan downed Michigan State 45-28.

Oct. 16 – Calgary Stampeders of the CFL place Howard on their negotiating list.

Oct. 19 – Caught three TD passes in a 24-16 win over Indiana, tying the Michigan single-game mark for the second time in the season.

Oct. 25 – Caught TD passes of 65 and 41 yards in a 52-6 win at Minnesota, giving him 15 pass reception touchdowns for the season, surpassing Anthony Carter's Big Ten record of 14.

Nov. 2 – Caught a pair of TD passes as Michigan downed Purdue 42-0. It was also the eighth consecutive game in which he'd scored at least two touchdowns.

Nov. 16 – Caught a one-yard TD pass from Grbac during a 20-0 shutout of Illinois, for a Big Ten single-season record of 19 TD pass receptions. It was also the 12th straight game overall and 11th consecutive game during the season in which he'd caught a touchdown pass, both NCAA records. The 19 TD passes from Grbac to Howard also tied an NCAA season mark for a pass reception tandem.

Nov. 23 – Set a Michigan record with a 93-yard punt return TD during the Wolverines' 31-3 win over Ohio State, striking a Heisman Trophy pose after he reached the end zone. Finished with 90 points in conference games to become the first receiver to lead the Big Ten in scoring. His overall total of 138 points also set a Michigan single-season record.

Nov. 25 – Named to the Football Writers Association of America All-America team.

Nov. 27 – Won the Walter Camp Award as the most outstanding player in college football.

Dec. 5 – Named to Associated Press All-America team.

Dec. 7 – Won the Maxwell Award as the nation's top college football player, garnering 74 percent of the vote.

Dec. 8 – Won the Paul Warfield Award as the NCAA's top receiver.

Dec. 10 – Named to the United Press International All-America team.

Dec. 14 – Won the Heisman Trophy, garnering the second-largest margin of victory in the 57-year history of the award.

1992

Jan. 13 – Finished ninth in voting for AP Athlete of the Year, garnering two first-place votes.

Jan. 21 – Announced he would leave Michigan and enter the NFL draft.

April 26 – Selected fourth overall by the Washington Redskins in the NFL draft.

June 20 – Named Big Ten Athlete of the Year.

Aug. 25 – Signed his first pro contract, a four-year deal with Washington.

Sept. 13 – Scored his first NFL touchdown when Brian Mitchell pitched back a punt return that Howard took 55-yards for a score in Washington's 24-17 victory over the Atlanta Falcons at RFK Stadium.

Nov. 15 – Had a season-long 42-yard kick return at Kansas City's Arrowhead Stadium.

Dec. 26 – Got first career start in regular-season finale at RFK Stadium. But left the game early with a separated shoulder while making a catch.

Dec. 30 – Placed on Injured Reserve with shoulder injury. Missed Redskins' two playoff games.

1993

Oct. 10 – Had his first NFL multi-reception game of his career when he hauled in three passes in a 41-7 loss to the New York Giants at RFK Stadium.

Dec. 31 – Had his biggest receiving game of his NFL career to date, with six catches for 68 yards in a 14-9 loss to the Minnesota Vikings at RFK Stadium.

1994

Sept. 4 – Caught his first NFL TD pass, a 27-yard strike from quarterback John Friesz during Washington's 28-7 loss to the Seattle Seahawks at RFK Stadium.

1995

Feb. 15 – Selected by Jacksonville Jaguars in NFL expansion draft.

Oct. 1 – Caught a 15-yard scoring pass from Mark Brunell with 1:03 left to play as Jacksonville edged the Houston Oilers 17-16 for the first victory in Jaguars' franchise history.

1996

July 11 – Signed by Green Bay Packers as a free agent.

Dec. 15 – Returned a punt 92 yards for a TD in Green Bay's 31-3 win over Detroit, then struck the Heisman pose in the end zone of the Pontiac Silverdome as he celebrated. It was his third return TD as a Packer, which is both a franchise single-season, and career, record.

Dec. 22 - Finished the season with an NFL single-season record of 875 punt return yards, shattering Fulton Walker's previous mark of 692 yards.

1997

Jan. 4 – Returned a punt 71 yards for a TD during a 35-14 win over San Francisco in the NFC Divisional playoff game at Lambeau Field.

Jan. 12 – Had four kick returns and one punt return for a combined 107 yards in the Packers' 30-13 win over Carolina in the NFC Championship at Lambeau Field.

Jan. 26 – Set a Super Bowl record with a 99-yard kick return for a TD and became the first special teams player to be named Super Bowl MVP and just the fourth player to win both the Heisman Trophy and Super Bowl MVP as the Packers dropped the New England Patriots 35-21 in Super Bowl XXXI.

March 5 – Signed as a free agent with the Oakland Raiders.

March 17 – Appeared as himself in a guest spot on the popular television sitcom, "Everybody Loves Raymond".

1999

June 8 – Released by the Oakland Raiders.

June 23 – Signed as a free agent by the Green Bay Packers.

Dec. 1 – Released by the Green Bay Packers.

Dec. 4 – Signed as a free agent by the Detroit Lions.

Dec. 5 – In his debut with the Lions, returned a punt 68 yards for a TD, sparking Detroit's 33-17 win over Washington, the first victory by the Lions over the Redskins since Oct. 3, 1965.

2000

Sept. 3 – Returned a punt 95 yards for a score in Detroit's 14-10 season-opening victory at New Orleans, on the same field where he was named Super Bowl MVP.

2001

Oct. 21 – Scored his final NFL TD on a 36-yard pass from Charlie Batch in Detroit's 27-24 loss to the Tennessee Titans. It was his first TD catch since 1995.

Oct. 28 – Set a career high with 229 yards in kickoff returns during Detroit's 31-27 loss to the Cincinnati Bengals.

2003

Feb. 25 – Released by Detroit Lions.

2005

Jan. 1 – Inducted into the Gator Bowl Hall of Fame.

Feb. 2 – Took to the track in the Richard Petty Driving Experience at the Daytona International Speedway, hitting speeds in excess of 100 mph.

May 6 – Selected to appear on the cover of EA Sports NCAA Football 06 for both the Playstation 2 and Xbox video game systems.

Sept. 3 - Joined the staff of ESPN's "College GameDay".

Sept. 22 – Inducted into the Greater Cleveland Sports Hall of Fame.

2006

May 1 – Named the cover athlete for EA Sports NCAA Football 06 video game. Cover art showed Howard striking his Heisman pose after his famous punt return TD against Ohio State in 1991.

2008

Feb. 9 – Inducted into the University of Michigan's Hall of Honor.

Feb. 11 – Inducted into the Michigan Sports Hall of Fame during a ceremony at Detroit's Max M. Fisher Music Center.

2009

Jan. 8 – Was one of 10 former Orange Bowl winners recognized during the 2009 National Championship game between Oklahoma and Florida

June 26 – Named the ninth greatest return man in NFL history by the NFL Network.

2010

Feb. 22-27 – Participated along with ESPN football analysts Herm Edwards, Mark Schlereth and Mark May in an episode of ABC'S "Extreme Makeover: Home Edition", filmed in Pine Mountain Valley, GA.

May 28 – Announced as a member of the College Football Hall of Fame's class of 2011.

Sept. 10 – Selected by the Big Ten Network as the conference's 34th-best student-athlete of all-time as part of the "Big Ten Icons" series.

Dec. 7 – Honored for his induction into the College Football Hall of Fame during a reception at New York's Waldorf Astoria Hotel.

Dec. 14 – Big Ten Conference announces its annual award to the top receiver will be named the Richter-Howard Receiver of the Year in honor of Howard and former Wisconsin wideout Pat Richter.

2011

Jan. 5 – Sports Illustrated cites Howard's kick return TD as the decisive moment of Super Bowl XXXI.

Feb. 17 – Named to USA Football's board of directors.

July 16 – Officially inducted into the College Football Hall of Fame during ceremonies in South Bend, IN.

HEISMAN
LEGENDS
AT
MICHIGAN

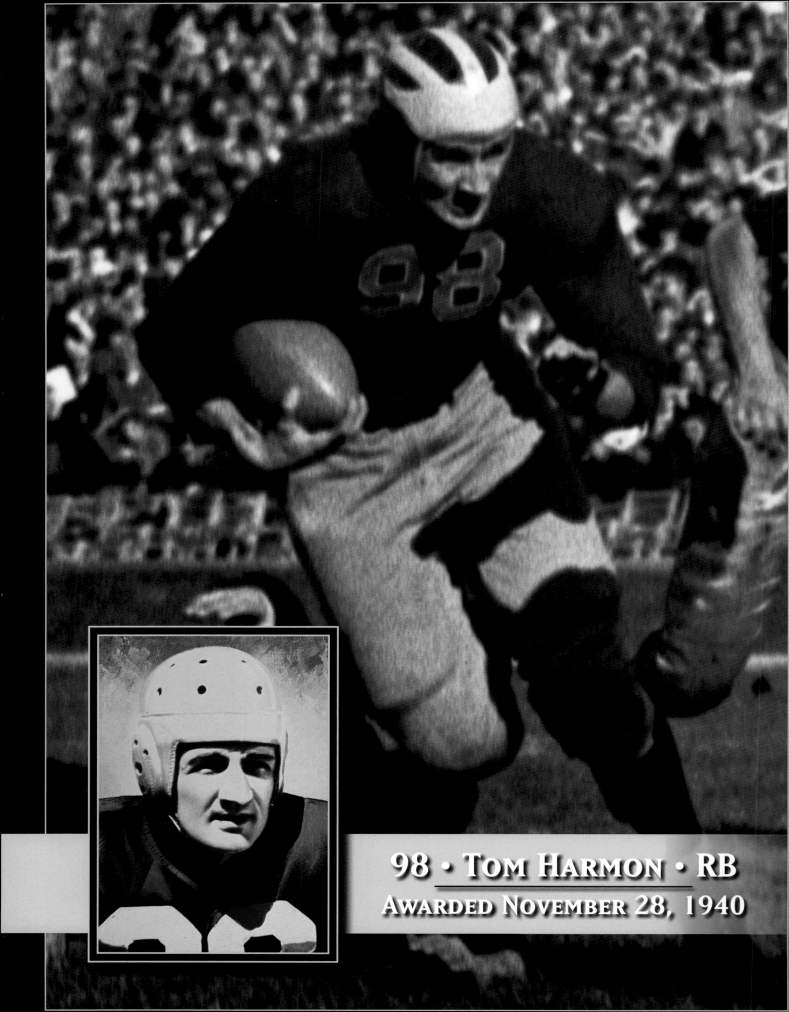

98 • TOM HARMON • RB
AWARDED NOVEMBER 28, 1940

21 · DESMOND HOWARD · WR
AWARDED DECEMBER 14, 1991

2 · CHARLES WOODSON · DB
AWARDED DECEMBER 13, 1997